PAUL'S JOURNEYS

Copyright © Peter Trevvett 2013

First published in Great Britain in 2013 by Onefocus EU Limited, Welcome House, Falkland Close, Coventry CV4 8AU

ISBN: 978-0-9575052-0-9

A CIP catalogue record for this book is available from the British Library

Design and maps by R+H Design, Lancaster

Printed and bound by Butler Tanner and Dennis Ltd using vegetable based inks on FSC sourced paper

PAUL'S JOURNEYS

Troubles and dangers without
Incessant anxieties within
A courage that quailed before no peril
A love for poor sinners and for the assembly
that nothing chilled

A Portrayal of Paul by
J.N. Darby, 1800–1882

INTRODUCTION

Paul is the most extraordinary figure in Christianity after Christ. Taken from the heart of Judaism to become apostle to the Gentiles his conversion was the greatest ever, yet a pattern for every believer.

Totally devoted to the service of his Master he endured incessant opposition, stoning, scourging, shipwreck, imprisonment and finally martyrdom. Yet, almost single-handed, he brought the light of Christianity to the west, and his nine letters to the assemblies he served, plus four to individuals, are part of the canon of Scripture and comprise almost half of the New Testament – more than half if we include Hebrews.

This book traces what we know of his stupendous journeys. We hope you find it interesting – even inspiring

NOTES

SOURCES The only primary sources are Luke's account in Acts of the Apostles, and Paul's epistles, particularly Galatians.

The extraordinary accuracy of Acts of the Apostles has been proved many times. The distinguished New Testament scholar Sir William Ramsay (1851–1939), who spent many years in Asia Minor, started his researches doubting its veracity. After a lifetime of research, however, he concluded:

> *Further study... showed that the book could bear the most minute scrutiny as an authority for the facts of the Aegean world, and that it was written with such judgement, skill, art and perception for truth as to be a model of historical statement... You may press the words of Luke in a degree beyond any other historian's and they stand the keenest scrutiny and the hardest treatment.*
>
> ('The bearing of recent discovery on the trustworthiness of the New Testament')

ROUTES Sometimes Luke gives routes in considerable detail. At other times he can compress large distances into a couple of verses. Often routes taken by the apostle and his companions are uncertain, and this is indicated in the text and on the maps.

DISTANCES including sea travel, are mostly given in statute miles (English miles) and kilometres. For a comparison with nautical and Roman miles please refer to the marginal note in chapter 2. All distances given are approximate and are based on probable routes.

PICTURES have been chosen that omit modern buildings and other works, to give an idea of the terrain in Paul's day. The march of twenty centuries has left its impress: coastlines have eroded, estuaries and harbours have silted up and above all the constructions of man have crumbled. It is nevertheless remarkable how many Roman and Greek ruins survive, and how many Roman roads still exist.

NOTES

MEANINGS of uncommon words and explanations of names are given in the **GLOSSARY**, page 136.

SCRIPTURES Quotations are from the New Translation by J.N. Darby.

CONTENTS

SECTION 1

TRAVEL IN PAUL'S DAY

ALL ROADS LEAD TO ROME

CHAPTER

1

The Roman road system was perhaps the greatest factor which made Paul's amazing journeys possible.

Rome relied on its roads. The empire was built on military power and Roman roads meant armies could be moved to where they were needed – and quickly. When the empire declined and fell the same roads also gave access to the invaders, but that is another story. Then there was trade. The bulk of imports came by sea, but roads were also important. The city of Rome had an enormous appetite for every kind of commodity, as well as food. Luxuries from the east, slaves, prisoners and wild animals for the *venationes*, and marble for building projects in Rome were all transported along the Roman *viae*.

But the main purpose of the Roman road system was communication. The Roman Empire was vast and sprawling. It stretched from England to Egypt. There were many different nations, peoples, religions and languages. At one time there were one hundred and thirteen provinces and rapid communication between them was vital if government was to be upheld. So, when the empire superseded the Republic, Augustus set up the Imperial Post, the *cursus publicus*, to transport messages, officials and tax revenues between provinces, which depended on a chain of stations – *mansions* – along the major roads. These provided relays of horses, vehicles for magistrates and other officials, mules, fodder and accommodation. The imperial messengers averaged around 45 miles (72 km) a day. This service, however, was not available for private correspondence. No doubt Paul's epistles would have been carried to their destinations by trusted friends.

All roads lead to Rome, it is said – and this was true, at least before Constantinople became capital of the empire. At one time no fewer than twenty-nine great highways radiated from the city like spokes in a wheel. Their hub was the *miliarius aurem*, a golden zero milestone erected in the *Forum*. There were two hundred and fifty thousand miles of Roman roads,

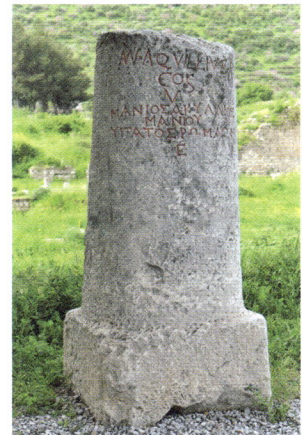

Our word mile comes from the Latin *milic passuum*, meaning one thousand paces. So a Roman mile was 4,860 feet (1,620 yards, 1,481 metres) and was marked by a milestone, a mililiaria, like this one at Ephesus. A milestone was a round stone column on a rectangular base set more than two feet (61 cm) into the ground and standing some five feet (1.5 metres) high, inscribed with the number of the mile, and other information. After Augustus became superintendent of the road system of Rome and its environs, in 20 BC, he set up the golden milestone, miliarius aurem, in the Forum at Rome, and all roads were considered as starting from this monument.

THE
ROADS
OF THE
ROMAN
EMPIRE

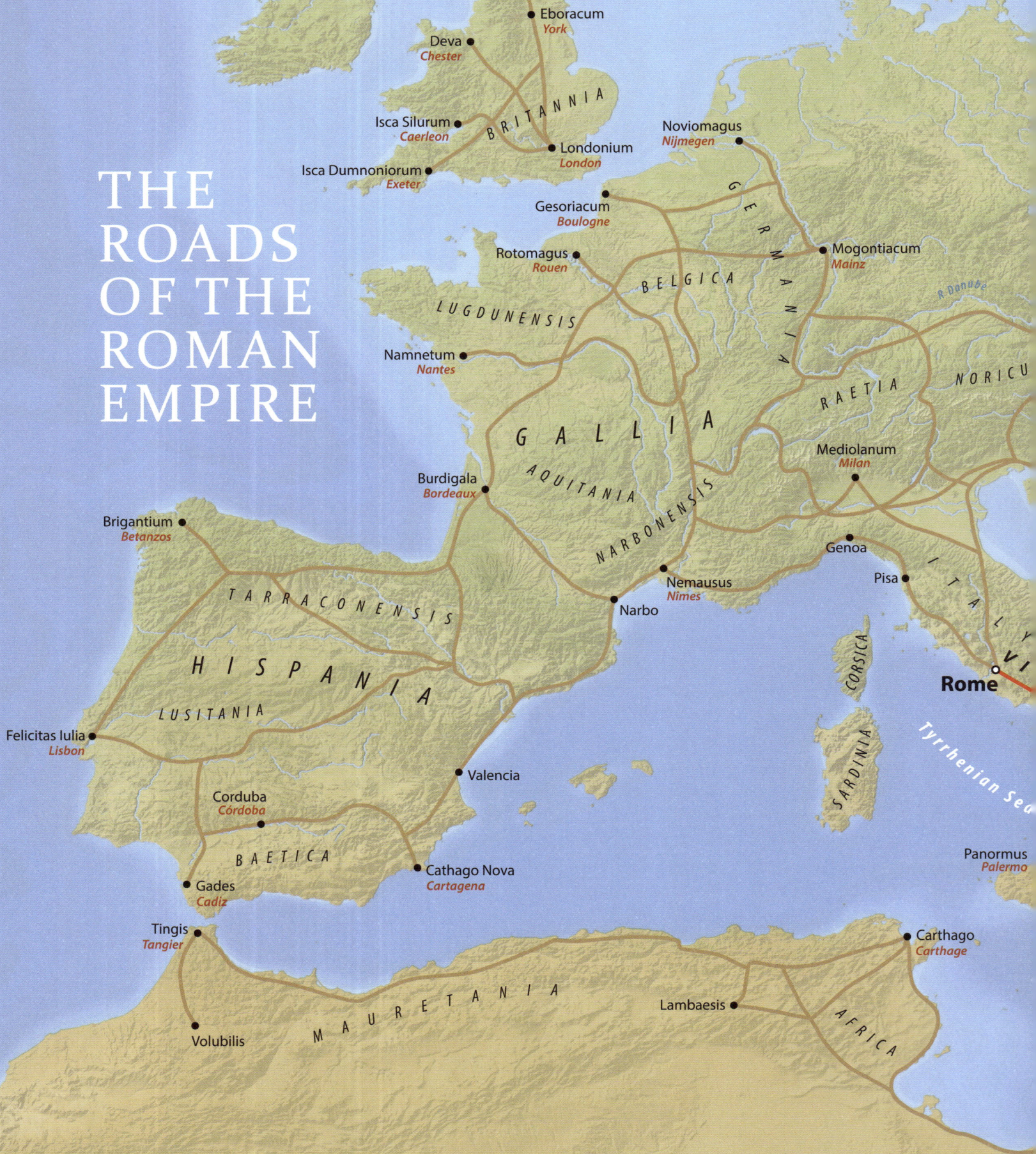

Eboracum
York

Deva
Chester

Isca Silurum
Caerleon

BRITANNIA

Isca Dumnoniorum
Exeter

Londonium
London

Noviomagus
Nijmegen

Gesoriacum
Boulogne

Rotomagus
Rouen

GERMANIA

Mogontiacum
Mainz

BELGICA

R. Donube

LUGDUNENSIS

Namnetum
Nantes

RAETIA

NORICU

GALLIA

AQUITANIA

Burdigala
Bordeaux

NARBONENSIS

Mediolanum
Milan

Genoa

Brigantium
Betanzos

Nemausus
Nîmes

Pisa

TARRACONENSIS

Narbo

ITALY

HISPANIA

CORSICA

Rome

LUSITANIA

Felicitas Iulia
Lisbon

Tyrrhenian Sea

Valencia

SARDINIA

Corduba
Córdoba

BAETICA

Panormus
Palermo

Gades
Cadiz

Cathago Nova
Cartagena

Tingis
Tangier

Carthago
Carthage

MAURETANIA

Lambaesis

AFRICA

Volubilis

PANNONIA

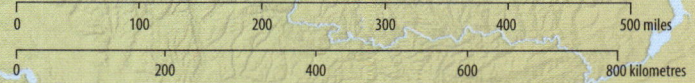

Aquincum
Budapest

DALMATIA

DACIA

MOESIA

Adriatic Sea

PPIA

eapolis
aples

Brundisium
Brindisi

Dyrrachium
Durrës

MACEDONIA

EPIRUS

VIA EGNATIA

Philippi

Thessalonica
Thessaloniki

THRACE

Byzantium
Istanbul

BITHYNIA

BLACK SEA

Trapesus

ARMENIA

GALATIA

CAPPADOCIA

Troas

Pergamum

ASIA

Iconium
Konya

Tarsus

CILICIA

Antioch

SYRIA

Ionian Sea

Rhegium
*Reggio di
Calabria*

CILY

Syracuse

MALTA

ACHAIA

Patrae
Patras

Corinth

Athens

Aegean Sea

Ephesus

LYCIA

Attalia
Antalya

CYPRUS

Tyre

PHOENICIA

CRETE

MEDITERRANEAN SEA

Jerusalem

JUDEA

Petra

Cyrene
Shahhat

CYRENAICA

Alexandria

ARABIA

EGYPT

3

| 0 | 100 | 200 | 300 | 400 | 500 miles |
| 0 | 200 | 400 | 600 | 800 kilometres |

one fifth of them paved. The functioning of the provinces depended on this nexus. But construction of these roads, although the Romans did not realise it, was allowed providentially for the spread of the gospel. Christianity reached Puteoli and Rome without a visit from an apostle, so far as we know. The gospel must have spread from Syria and Cilicia along the great routes that led to Italy, by Ephesus, Corinth and the sea, or overland by Troas, Philippi and the *Via Egnatia*.

A Roman bridge on the *Via Sebaste* 32 miles (51 km) west of Iconium.

Paul's roads

These were the roads used by Paul and his companions. On his first missionary journey (see chapter 7) the apostle visited Derbe, Lystra, Iconium and Antioch of Pisidia. These were important cities on the great central trade route which linked Italy to Cappadocia, Syria and the east. From Antioch of Pisidia the route ran westward to Ephesus, and then by sea to Italy. Or the land route would take you by way of Troas, Philippi and Thessalonica to the Adriatic. When Paul and his companions left Philippi for Macedonia (see chapter 10) they headed west along the *Via Egnatia*, which ran from Byzantium (modern Istanbul) to Dyrrhachium on the Adriatic coast (see page 61). Travellers crossing from there to Brindisium could then follow the *Via Appia* straight to Rome. So the *Via Egnatia* was Rome's main link to her eastern Mediterranean provinces. More importantly, it enabled Paul to take his glad tidings to Thessalonica and elsewhere, and this is probably the road he would have used when he went to Illyricum (see page 81).

Several forms of conveyance were available to travellers. The humblest was the ass, then mules and horses. Officials might travel in litters borne by slaves. Then there were various types of carriage: these might be two or four wheeled, heavy or light, and elaborately painted and cushioned coaches for the rich. It was often possible to hire carriages with mules or horses from one stage to the next.

We cannot usually tell from Scripture when Paul and his companions travelled on foot, and when they hired beasts. On Paul's last visit to Judea the journey from Caesarea to Jerusalem, a distance of 62 miles (100 km), appears to have taken two days, with luggage (Acts 21: 15–17). If so, horses and perhaps carriages must have been used. But whatever the mode of travel the apostle's stamina was hardly believable. After being stoned at Lystra, and taken up as dead, he set off with Barnabas for Derbe, which was about 85 miles (137 km) from Lystra. From Philippi, after being

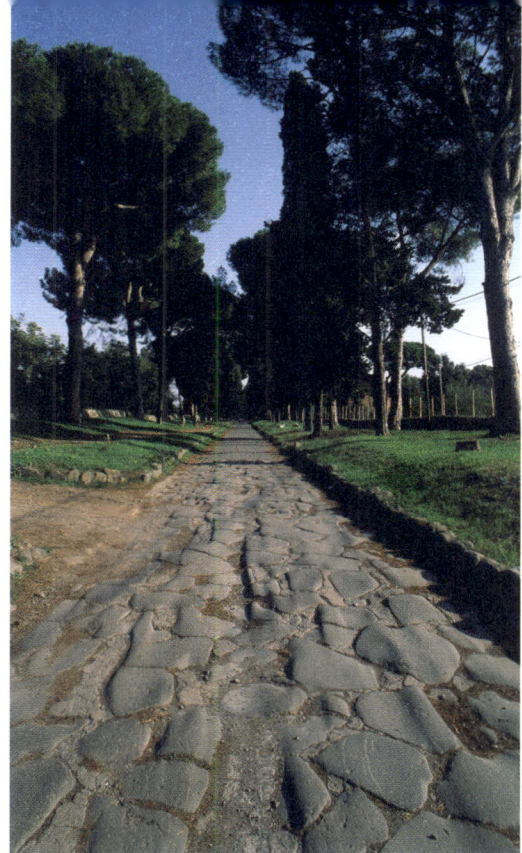

The Appian Way, most famous of Roman roads, ran 125 miles (201 km) south east from Rome to Capua, near Naples, then across Italy to Brundisium, the port for the east. Paul was taken to Rome as a prisoner along this ancient highway after landing at Puteoli (Acts 28: 14, 15). Built in 312 BC to allow movement of troops during the Samnite Wars, it ran on a causeway for 19 miles (31 km) across the treacherous Pontine Marshes.

THE ENGINEERING OF A ROMAN ROAD

Roman roads were first built around 500 BC. They allowed the rapid movement of armies and goods, which were so vital in building military and economic strength. This made all the difference to the development of the state. Often roads were named after their constructors such as Appia and Cassia. Roman determination is reflected in their design. They invariably confronted obstacles rather than go round them. They built causeways, cuttings, bridges and tunnels so that the roads could run in lines of uncompromising straightness. The principal roads – main roads and military highways – were paved with blocks of stone, with a camber for drainage, cemented with mortar. These were laid over a deep foundation of sand and gravel in an excavated ditch, or *fossa*. They were built to last, with minimum maintenance. Roman skills in road building were lost in the Middle Ages, like many of their technical achievements. They were not revived until the nineteenth century.

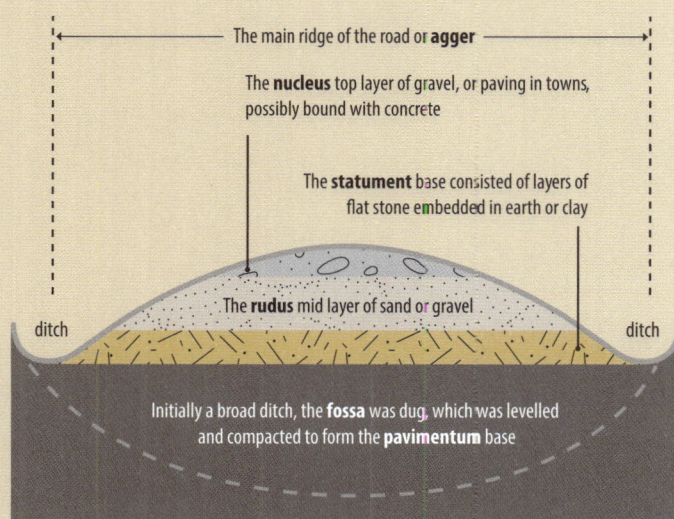

The main ridge of the road or **agger**

The **nucleus** top layer of gravel, or paving in towns, possibly bound with concrete

The **statument** base consisted of layers of flat stone embedded in earth or clay

The **rudus** mid layer of sand or gravel

ditch

ditch

Initially a broad ditch, the **fossa** was dug, which was levelled and compacted to form the **pavimentum** base severely beaten and spending a night in prison, which included an earthquake, the apostle departed, undaunted, for Thessalonica. And he chose to walk the 30 miles (48 km) to Assos alone, after the long discourse at Troas, and a sleepless night of great intensity.

Travellers on foot could reckon to cover around 15 to 18 miles (24 to 29 km) a day. Not many could sustain much over 3 miles an hour (5 km an hour) with some luggage, for more than 5 or 6 hours. This was especially so in the hot season. A typical day's march for Roman infantry was 20 miles (32 km). When Paul was escorted from Jerusalem to Antipatris (Acts 23: 31) the distance was 35 miles (56 km), which was unusually long for a continuous march.

Road travel involved some danger. The biggest was robbery. It was extensive during the Republic but ruthlessly suppressed by the emperors. The penalty for a robber was crucifixion (see Matthew 27: 38). The *Pax Romana* during the rule of Augustus led to a great increase in travel, but security was still weak in mountainous and remote areas such as parts of Cilicia. This must have been an important consideration when large sums of money for Judea were conveyed by Paul and his company. Paul also refers to being *in perils of rivers*. In mountainous regions watercourses could become raging torrents with very little warning and travellers who were not swept away risked being cut off. Travel was restricted in the winter months when the high passes were blocked with snow, and in heavy rain high ground such as the Taurus plateau could be transformed into an impassable sea of mud.

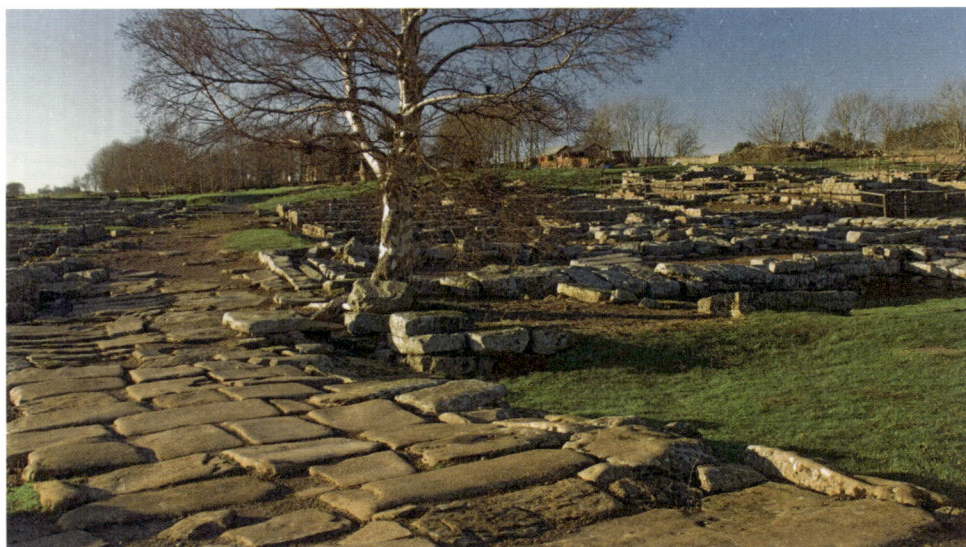

Via Praetoria, a paved Roman roadway at Vinolanda, Roman Wall south, Northumbria, England.

SEA TRAVEL

The Romans were slow to adopt sea travel.
However they were forced to form a navy
to combat the warships operated by their
enemy, Carthage. Hannibal might never
have thought of marching his armies over
the Alps had it not been for Rome's control
of the Tuscan Sea, to the north of Corsica.
After the Punic Wars Sextus Pompeius, who
fought with Mark Antony against Octavian,
built up a powerful navy, based at Marseille,
and gained control of Sicily, preventing
grain ships from reaching Rome. His defeat
off Naulochus, Sicily, and the defeat of
Anthony and Cleopatra off the Gulf of Actium in the Ionian Sea in 31 BC,
gave Italy supremacy over the Mediterranean, which the Romans called *mare
nostrum* – our sea.

St Paul's Bay on the island of Rhodes, where Paul's ship called on the last stage of his third great journey.

Sea travel increased greatly during the first and second centuries. The
seas were important to appease Rome's insatiable hunger for food and
commodities. The ports of Ostia and Puteoli received ships from Cadiz with
cargoes of wool, vessels from the west and also traders from Sicily, which was
known as the storehouse of Italy. There were sailings to and from Corinth,
and Carthage. After Egypt was annexed to Rome in 30 BC Alexandria became
a transit port for spices, dyes and perfumes from the Far East, as well as
exports from Egypt itself. And goods conveyed along the great northern land
route had to be transhipped to the capital from Ephesus or Dyrrachium.

The sailing season
The seas were closed – *Mare clausum* – between 10th November and 10th
March. The safe sailing season was shorter still, from 26th May to 14th
September. For the Romans March 5th was the starting date following the

CHAPTER 2

SEA TRAVEL   7

festival of *Navigium Isidis*. Few were bold enough to sail in the winter months. Apart from the risk of bad weather, overcast skies made navigation problematic as the sun or stars were relied on to plot a course. Sailing was also governed by the winds. In the eastern Mediterranean the Etesian winds blew steadily from the northwest throughout the summer months.

Sea travel was dangerous. Piracy flourished in the eastern Mediterranean after the Punic Wars, especially in Cilicia and Crete. It was effectively eliminated by Gnaeus Pompeius Magnus, better known as Pompey, military and political leader in the late Roman republic, and member of the First Triumvirate. In 67 BC he quartered the Mediterranean with five hundred ships, clearing out the pirates and destroying 1,300 of their vessels in just forty days. A greater risk, in Paul's day, was the ships themselves. The pressure of storms and heavy seas could strain the ship's timbers causing leaks and if these became too great the ship simply broke up. This may have been what happened when Paul spent a night and a day in the deep (2 Corinthians 11: 25). In such a circumstance the likelihood of being picked up by another vessel was remote. Sailing ships were difficult to manoeuvre and saving lives was not given high priority. Paul also tells the Corinthians he had suffered shipwreck three times, and that was before the shipwreck described in Acts 27.

> *... three times I have suffered shipwreck, a night and day I passed in the deep...*
>
> **2 Corinthians 11: 25**

The site of the harbour at Seleucia Piria, the port for Antioch in Syria. Paul, Barnabas and Mark embarked here for Cyprus on the apostle's first western journey (Acts 13: 4). The line of the southern breakwater can be seen below the distant mountains.

Sailing ships

Merchant ships had a length to width ratio of 3 or 4 to 1. They usually relied on a large, square mainsail, made of hemp and coloured and painted with devices, and a single mast. This put great leverage on the hull. Damage to the timbers could be caused by a gale, which may have happened after

Paul's ship was blown from Crete to Clauda by the hurricane *Euroclydon*. A boat, for use in the event of shipwreck or shore landings, was towed behind. The single sail was ideal for running before the wind, but not so suitable for tacking. Ancient ships could go no closer to the wind than 7 or 8 points (7 or 8 times 11° 15'). Steering was by side rudders, or steering oars, located at the stern quarters, controlled by a tiller. The steersman often stood on the roof of the cabin, in the stern.

Sea travel was much quicker than going by land. A favourable wind might allow an average speed of four or five knots. Pliny the elder gave a time of nine days for a voyage from Puteoli to Alexandria, in Egypt, a distance of 1,050 nautical miles (1,209 statute miles, 1,945 km) which gives an average speed of 4.9 knots (1,050 miles/9 days x 24 hours). Obviously there must have been a following wind. Ships heading south during the summer months often had the wind behind them but for ships heading north it was a different story. A typical voyage time from Alexandria to Puteoli was more likely fifteen to twenty days.

Accommodation was mostly on merchant ships. There were no special facilities for passengers. Coasting vessels, *orariis navibus*, sailed from one port to another along the coasts taking advantage of offshore breezes and currents. Sea-going vessels were much larger. According to Josephus there were 600 passengers on board a ship taking prisoners from Judea to Rome. When Paul left Troas (Acts 20) he evidently sailed in a coasting vessel which stopped for the night at Mitylene, Chios, Samos and other places, before boarding a larger vessel at Patara which took him all the way to Tyre.

Grain ships

The ship boarded by the centurion and his prisoners at Myra was a grain ship. Grain was of the utmost importance to Rome, as the basic food source of the population. This was partly a problem of Rome's own making. As the empire expanded the influx of wealth changed agriculture so that great capitalist ranches sprang up, operated by slaves, and thousands of displaced peasant farmers swarmed into Rome in a vain attempt to find work. There are similarities with the Russian Communist collectivisation programme of the 1930s, except that the Roman peasants were not slaughtered or left to die, but became a burden on the state. In the time of Julius Caesar as many as three hundred and twenty thousand citizens were receiving free corn but Augustus reduced the number to two hundred thousand.

1 knot =
1 nautical mile per hour (1.15 statute (or English) miles, 1.85 km)

1 nautical mile =
1.151 English miles (6,076 feet, 1.85 km)

1 Roman mile =
0.92 English miles (4,860 feet, 1.48 km)

The stability of the empire depended on supplies getting through, otherwise this underclass might form an anarchist mob. So grain transportation from Egypt, the main producing country, was effectively under state control, with contracts between the Imperial government and private owners, or trading companies. There had been some terrible winter famines during Caligula's reign, and Claudius, the fourth Roman emperor, was mobbed by a hungry crowd during a bread shortage, forcing him to enter his palace by the back door. Fear of grain supplies running out added to the pressure for winter navigation. The ship which carried Paul as a prisoner from Myra to Malta was travelling late in the season, its owner evidently hoping to profit from an extra voyage.

According to a fourth century source Egypt sent one hundred and forty thousand tonnes of grain to Rome in the time of Augustus. As the empire became established, and the population of Rome exceeded one million, the annual grain requirement has been calculated at four hundred and twenty thousand tonnes. This would have required twelve hundred large ships with an average capacity of three hundred and fifty tonnes. This works out at around five vessels per navigable day. Of course, many ships had smaller capacity, but some could hold five hundred tonnes, or even more.

Large ships could not approach the river port of Ostia and had to put in at Puteoli. Their cargoes were then transhipped by smaller vessels. And even after unloading at Ostia the precious goods had to be loaded on to barges – *naves caudicariae* – and towed up the Tiber by animals or slaves.

Although the Romans introduced many technical developments, the compass was not one of them. It was first developed in China in the fourth century AD and not used in Europe until the 11th century.

Puteoli (modern Pozzuoli) in the Gulf of Naples, the usual port for large grain ships with cargoes for Rome.

The arrival of the grain fleet from Alexandria during the month of June was a significant event. These were the only ships permitted to enter the port of Puteoli without striking their topsails, so they could be seen from a distance. Escorted by war galleys the great vessels sailed majestically into the Bay of Naples to be welcomed by large, enthusiastic crowds.

SECTION 2

"AN ELECT VESSEL"

ACTS 9: 15

"A JEW, BORN IN TARSUS"

A number of different strands were interwoven in the tapestry of Paul's background. Above all, he was a Jew, and a Pharisee. But he was also a Roman citizen, as well as a citizen of Tarsus of Cilicia. He was born only a few years after Christ, but we have no indication that he ever saw the Lord, in the days of His flesh. However he would have been alive at the same time as Christ, John the Baptist and the disciples.

If anyone had told Saul's parents that their son would become a preacher to the nations, as well as to Israel, they would have indignantly refused the idea. Nevertheless his background providentially equipped him to approach persons from the three principal branches of the race, at that time. As a Hebrew, and a strict Pharisee, he understood the inner workings of Judaism. As a Greek citizen – a Hellenist – he could relate to much of the contemporary world. And as a Roman he was aware of the principles and power of the empire. Much later he would write to the Corinthians:

> For being free from all, I have made myself bondman to all, that I might gain the most possible. And I became to the Jews as a Jew, in order that I might gain the Jews: to those under law, as under law… in order that I might gain those under law: to those without law, as without law…in order that I might gain those without law. I became to the weak, as weak, in order that I might gain the weak. To all I have become all things, in order that at all events I might save some. (1 Corinthians 9: 19–22).

'A Jew'

Paul was born a Jew, and circumcised on the eighth day (Philippians 3: 5). He was of the race of Israel and of the seed of Abraham (2 Corinthians 11: 22) so was not of mixed stock, or a proselyte. What was more, he could trace his ancestry back to the tribe of Benjamin (Philippians 3: 5, Romans 11: 1), in contrast to many Jews in the first century who did not know their genealogy, or were descended from proselytes. Paul's tribe originated from the only patriarch actually born in the land of promise and was one of the tribes that returned to the land in Nehemiah's day.

Most likely his parents would have taught Paul the Old Testament Scriptures from an early age. Jewish boys were usually sent to elementary school connected with the synagogue, from the age of six, where they learned the law by oral repetition. The age of majority was thirteen. They would then participate in Sabbath services, and be responsible to follow Jewish ritual law, tradition and ethics. Thirteen was also the age when a Jewish boy destined to be a Rabbi enrolled in the school of a distinguished teacher.

Paul tells the Jews (Acts 22: 3) that although born in Tarsus he was brought up in Jerusalem, and he informs Agrippa (Acts 26: 4, 5) that his manner of life *from my youth, which from its commencement was passed among my nation in Jerusalem* was as a Pharisee. So he would have left Tarsus for Jerusalem at the age of twelve or thirteen, or even earlier to learn *at the feet of Gamaliel* (Acts 22: 3) or it may be the whole family moved there.

It seems without doubt that Judaism had a much greater influence on the great apostle's early development than secular Hellenism. His upbringing as a Pharisee would have been rigid. He would have been kept separate from the moral corruption that prevailed in Tarsus, and had no inclination to commit evil. This is confirmed by his assertion that he had walked in all good conscience with God (Acts 23: 1) and that he was found blameless as to righteousness which is in the law (Philippians 3: 6). And in Romans 3: 8 the apostle refutes the slander that his doctrine allowed evil. The culture of a leading Hellenist city may have influenced his early years, but Paul's written Greek, although fluent and powerful, is in his own style, and does not betray a classical education, or undue familiarity with the great poets, although he does quote the Cretan poet Epimenedes (Acts 17: 28, Titus 1: 12) and the Cilician poet Aratus (Acts 17: 28).

A Hebrew

Paul also describes himself as *Hebrew of Hebrews* (Philippians 3: 5). The word was used to designate Jews of Jerusalem and Judea, who could still speak Hebrew (Aramaic), as opposed to the Hellenist Jews dispersed throughout the Mediterranean lands, who spoke the Greek of their adopted countries.

Despite Paul's status as a Hebrew, it has been said the Hebrews were not his natural sphere (J.N. Darby, Synopsis, volume 4, page 27). The differences between the two branches of Judaism involved more than just language. The Aramaic speaking Jews of Judea looked askance on the Hellenists, regarding them as influenced by Greek culture. By the first century AD Jews had settled in nearly every country of the civilised world and an estimated eighty-five per cent were Hellenists. Being a Hebrew would therefore imply a certain distinction. Jews were recognised by the Romans as a distinct body until Vespasian ended their legal status once for all in 70 AD.

A Pharisee

Several times Paul refers to himself as a Pharisee, and also that he was a son of Pharisees (Acts 23: 6). As he reminded Agrippa, this was the strictest sect of the Jewish religion, whose adherents were marked by superior devotion, sanctity and knowledge of the law. The parable in Luke 18 shows how Pharisees looked down on persons whose moral standards they considered inferior.

A citizen of Tarsus

When he was persuading the Roman chiliarch to let him speak to the crowd in Jerusalem (Acts 21: 39) Paul referred to Tarsus as *no insignificant city of Cilicia*. Its origins are ancient, and it was inhabited in succession by Hittites, Greeks, Assyrians and Persians, taken by Alexander the Great, and then ruled by Seleucus I. Tarsus became part of the Roman Empire under Pompey in 67 BC, after he had used its harbour as a base to suppress piracy in the eastern Mediterranean. It was made a free city, *urbs libera*, in 44 BC and

A nineteenth century print of Tarsus.

was capital of the Roman province of Cilicia until 25 BC when the eastern part, which included Tarsus, was transferred to Syria. Cicero, the Roman statesman and philosopher, lived in Tarsus in 51 to 50 BC, when he was governor of the province and it was at Tarsus that Mark Anthony had his fateful meeting with Cleopatra in 41 BC.

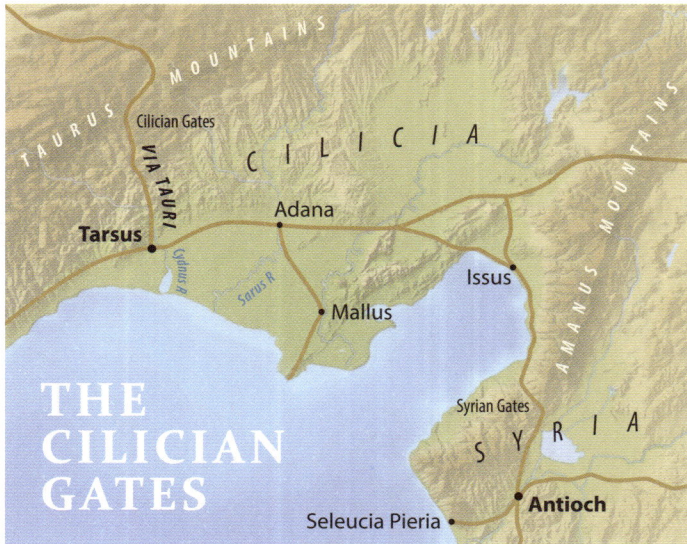

The setting of Tarsus in Paul's day must have been impressive, although there is scant evidence in any of his writings that he took much account of natural grandeur. Set in a fertile plain beneath the snow capped Taurus Mountains it was linked to the sea, 10 miles (16 km) away, by the river Cydnus. The city was well placed. The Cydnus was navigable by small vessels, and a lake served as a natural harbour which fully loaded ships could enter from the Mediterranean. Tarsus also controlled the 'Cilician Gates' about 27 miles (43 km) to the north which gave access to one of the few passes through the mountains, used by such figures in history as Xerxes, Darius, Cyrus the Younger and Alexander the Great as they mobilised their armies for conquest. So Tarsus was strategically situated on the main route between Syria and central Asia Minor, as well as being a centre for coastal traffic.

The Taurus mountains, north of Tarsus. The city was strategically important because the route through these mountains by the Cilician Gates pass gave access to the cities of Asia and the central plain.

Tarsus became Hellenised after Alexander's conquests. It was pagan and depraved, but also a centre of Greek culture and philosophy, especially Stoicism, with celebrated schools of learning. In the time of Seleucid I their library was said to have held 200,000 books, with a large collection of scientific works. Strabo, the first century geographer, declared that in philosophy and general education Tarsus was ahead of both Athens and Alexandria.

Paul was a *citizen* of Tarsus, a status he would have inherited from his father. The privilege depended on ancestry, not residence, and enrolment as a citizen required substantial wealth, and property worth 500 drachmae (two years' wages). So it seems Paul's family had means.

A Roman

The world Paul moved in was dominated by the Roman power. It was still recovering from the dislocation of the Civil War which ended when Augustus became emperor in 27 BC. When Paul was about to be scourged (Acts 22: 25) he informed the chiliarch that he had inherited Roman citizenship. Tarsus was a regional capital in the Roman Empire, but living there did not convey a right to Roman *civitas*. It may have been awarded to his father or grandfather by an influential Roman in gratitude for some service, perhaps during the civil wars – a rare honour. Or it may have been bought (see Acts 22: 28). A more probable explanation is that Paul's father had been made a slave, like many Jews during the civil wars, and automatically received citizenship in the process of manumission, when freed by his Roman patron. A survey by the Emperor Claudius in 47 AD recorded fewer than six million Roman citizens out of a total population for the empire of around eighty million, so that Roman citizenship, however acquired, bestowed status and distinction. It also conferred important rights and protection under Roman law.

Yarn spun from Cilician goats' hair was woven into cilicium, the textile used in tent making.

PAUL'S TRADE

At some stage Paul would also have been taught a trade, the duty of every Jewish boy, as expressed by Gamaliel:

Learning of any kind unaccompanied by a trade ends in nothing, and leads to sin

In addition it was considered wrong to receive payment for imparting sacred knowledge, so that Rabbis were expected to be self supporting. Paul's trade was evidently tent-making, the raw material being cilicium, a textile woven locally from the abundant goats' hair harvested from the flocks of the Taurus. Without doubt his workmanship would have been of the highest standard and quality. One of the extraordinary features of the apostle's later service was his insistence on paying his way, by working with his hands to finance his great journeys (see chapter 10).

Paul's languages

These various strands are revealed in the languages Paul knew. Undoubtedly he knew Greek. It was the language he used to address the chiliarch, and the Athenians, and his epistles were written in *koine*, the everyday Greek of the time – with the possible exception of Hebrews. In these epistles he makes nearly 90 quotations – many of them apparently from memory – from the Septuagint. This was the Greek translation of the Hebrew Old Testament used by Hellenist Jews, and later by Christians, produced at Alexandria in the third century BC. Paul probably learned Greek as a boy, living in Tarsus, and some of the teaching under Gamaliel would have included Greek.

And he said, Dost thou know Greek?

Acts 21: 37, 38

Paul also quotes from the original Hebrew. It was in the Hebrew tongue that the Lord addressed him at his conversion, and the designation *Hebrew of Hebrews* (Philippians 3: 5) indicates that his family would have known Aramaic. This was the same Palestinian vernacular used by Jesus when in Manhood. It is believed to be the language, called Hebrew in Acts 21: 40 and Acts 22: 2, in which Paul addressed the Jewish crowd in Jerusalem, and the language spoken at Jerusalem during his education there.

It is likely Paul also knew Latin, the language of Imperial Rome, in which a Roman citizen was expected to be fluent. The hearing before Felix in Acts 24: 1–23 may have been conducted in Latin. Its knowledge would have been valuable for Paul during his confinement at Rome, and the judicial proceedings that took place there.

"An elect vessel"

Although the Lord did not intervene in Paul's life until the stoning of Stephen he was in the mind of God before he was born, indeed before the world was, and he was provided beforehand with the physical and mental qualities that would be needed for his great service. The Lord would describe him as *an elect vessel* (Acts 9: 15) and this vessel was prepared in advance before Paul was called.

THE EDUCATION OF A PHARISEE

Paul told the Jews at Jerusalem he had been *brought up in this city* (Acts 22: 3), and testified to Agrippa that his life had been spent in Jerusalem *from my youth*. Probably this meant from around thirteen years of age, or earlier. In any event, the day came in his life when he left Tarsus for the Holy City.

Tarsus to Jerusalem
410 miles (660 km) by sea,
480 miles (772 km) by land

The journey to Jerusalem

If Paul travelled by sea he would most likely have boarded a Phoenician or Greek trading ship, and landed at the new harbour of Caesarea Maritima, capital city of the Roman province of Palestine. It had been rebuilt by Herod the Great between 25 and 13 BC and named in honour of the Emperor Augustus. The alternative route by land would have taken some weeks: eastward across the Cilician plain, through the Syrian Gates, the pass through the Amanus mountains at a height of 2,165 feet (660 metres), descending to Antioch on the Orontes, starting point for Paul's future journeys, and down the narrow coastal plain to Caesarea.

Jerusalem was about two days' walk from Caesarea, and if the journey was in the time of a feast the road would have been crowded with pilgrims – up to one million attended major festivals. Approaching from the north the travellers would have seen the city of David set on a hill, with ranges of surrounding mountains, and the temple buildings on the eastern side.

David Tower, Jerusalem old city.

The Roman yoke

Paul may have found it stirring to pass through the land of his ancestors and view the Holy City, which he had doubtless been taught to revere from infancy. But once in Jerusalem he would be reminded that his people were under the domination of the Romans, and had been ever since Pompey entered the city in 63 BC. His invasion ended Jewish independence under the Hasmoneans, and he ignited a confrontational relationship with the Jews when he desecrated their temple. Herod the Great was appointed King of Judea in 37 BC and ruled, with Roman assent, until he died, probably in 1 AD. An Edomite by birth, he rebuilt Solomon's temple in magnificent style to placate the Jews, whose religion he had adopted. However he failed to win over the orthodox class: they did not forget how he had put to death the surviving Maccabees when he came to power, and slaughtered nearly every member of the Sanhedrim. And the tactless inclusion of a Roman eagle over the main Temple gate was a humiliating reminder of Gentile domination. The Antonia fortress, adjacent to the Temple buildings, where Paul would later be held as a prisoner, symbolised this clash of cultures, as did the presence of Roman soldiers in the streets and Temple precincts, and Roman coinage in the markets. In 6 AD Augustus had put Judea, Samaria and Idumea under the rule of a Roman procurator, and Caesarea replaced Jerusalem as the capital city. A further humiliation was that Judeans were required to pay personal tax direct to Caesar. No wonder the Jews looked for a saviour who would set them free.

The Jews

Two Jewish movements vied for leadership and position at this time. The Sadducees had the greatest power in the Sanhedrim, and monopolised the High Priesthood. They repudiated oral law (the tradition of the elders), did not believe in resurrection or a future state, and did not go out of their way to make disciples. The Pharisees, by contrast, were more numerous since they made proselytes (see Matthew 23: 15). They were also popular. The masses looked to them to preserve their national life and creed, and for relief from the intolerable chafing of the Roman yoke. Pharisees prided themselves on a superior sanctity of life marked by devotion to God and study of the law, and there were two principal schools: disciples of Shammai, an extreme rigorist, and followers of Hillel the Elder. Hillel was renowned for his wisdom and scholarship, and associated with the development of the Talmud, the primary source of Jewish religious law. And Gamaliel I, who taught Paul, was Hillel's grandson.

Gamaliel

Gamaliel was held in high renown by the Jews. Later Rabbis remembered him as the last of the great teachers:

> *When Rabban Gamaliel the Elder died, the glory of the law ceased and purity and abstinence died.* Mishnah (Sotah 9: 15)

He was the first to hold the title *Rabban* (master teacher), as opposed to *Rabbi* (my teacher). His advice to the Council not to put the disciples to death (Acts 5: 34–39) typified the tolerance of the Hillel school. His teaching was liberal and he even encouraged Greek learning. Rabbis traditionally sat raised above their students and Paul, at his feet, would have participated in free ranging discussion and dialectic, developing his skills in reasoning and debate as well as working at the exegesis of Scripture. However the main training in the Rabbinical schools was in the law. Pharisees believed the Babylonian captivity was because of failure to keep the Torah (the Mosaic Law), and its detailed study was therefore a duty. The scribes had identified 613 precepts in the written law, including 365 prohibitions and 248 positive commandments. In addition there were traditional customs handed down as oral teaching (see Mark 7: 13). The process of diligent analysis must have been an exacting discipline for a young man. It may be, as he worked at it, that Paul began to realise the inherent conflict between the holiness of the law and the innermost workings of his own nature, which he describes so vividly in Romans 7. However it was to be some time before he would find deliverance in Christ.

A Torah scroll with a silver yad pointing to the Hebrew words. The yad was used to avoid touching the sacred text with the fingers.

When Paul finished his education he would have been a trained Rabbi, steeped in knowledge of the law, and the Old Testament Scriptures. His brilliance and consistency would have made him a natural successor to Gamaliel. How long he stayed in Jerusalem, and whether he was there at the time of the crucifixion, we do not know. He first comes to light in Scripture at the death of Stephen.

"EXCEEDINGLY FURIOUS"

5

The early Jewish converts in Jerusalem continued to attend Jewish services in the temple, and practice Jewish ritual, at the same time as working out Christian fellowship (Acts 2: 42, 46). This situation still prevailed at the time of Paul's final visit, when the elders assured him that the believing Jews were all zealous of the law (Acts 21: 20). No doubt it remained so until the temple was finally destroyed by fire in the Roman invasion in 70 AD. This tended to blur the clear line between Christianity and Judaism. Some Jews, although they accepted the testimony of the apostles, regarded Christianity merely as a development of Judaism and failed to appreciate it was something entirely new. This was the seed of conflict within the church which was only partially resolved by the Acts 15 conference, and later grew into opposition against Paul, with attempts to undermine his Gentile assemblies. Stephen, however, stood out distinctively as one who had made a complete transfer to Christianity, and had a clear judgement of Judaism.

And, being exceedingly furious against them, I persecuted them even to cities out of our own land.
Acts 26: 11

The first Christian martyr

Stephen was one of the seven men appointed after the murmuring of the Hellenists (Greek speaking Jews) against the Hebrews. From their names it looks as if all seven were Hellenists. Stephen's faithful testimony brought him into conflict with members of various synagogues, including that of Cilicia, which Paul may well have attended. Before long he was brought before the Council, the Jewish Sanhedrim.

This was the highest Jewish tribunal. It was dominated by the Sadducean, priestly aristocracy but also included Pharisaic scribes and teachers and was under the presidency of the High Priest. Members sat in a semi circle facing the accused, and two clerks of court recorded votes for acquittal or condemnation.

Stephen appears to have been a young man, probably in his mid twenties. His skilful defence showed his detailed knowledge of the Scriptures, and refuted the charge that he had spoken against Moses. At the same time he exposed the history, in which the Jews so prided themselves, as one of opposition to God, pointing out the betrayal of Joseph, disloyalty to Moses, the people's involvement in idolatry and the despisal of the prophets. The anger of his audience would have been aroused when Stephen appeared to question the temple as a permanent centre of worship, and when he finally accused them of having been deliverers up and murderers of the Just One, implicating them in the history of resistance to the Holy Spirit, their fury erupted. Stephen was taken outside the city wall so that his blood would not be shed within Jerusalem, then stoned to death, praying for his executioners with his last breath.

So much for the Jews' detailed knowledge of the law! The trial was based on suborned witness. The procedure that condemnation should be delayed until the day following was ignored. And the Jews had in any case lost their power to impose the death penalty (see John 18: 31): an order for execution had to come from the Roman Governor, and the fact this was disregarded suggests that by this time Pontius Pilate had lost control over the province. So the whole proceedings were illegal, and amounted to lynch law.

'A young man called Saul'

Saul first comes to light in Scripture at the stoning of Stephen. It is not known if he stayed on in Jerusalem after his education under Gamaliel. The designation *young man* was used for ages between about twenty one and twenty eight, and Saul was possibly in his mid to late twenties at this time. According to the law (Deuteronomy 17: 7) the witnesses had to cast the first stones: to leave their arms free they took off their outer garments and laid them at Saul's feet.

The Jews lost no time in setting on a major persecution, in which Saul led. He showed none of the moderation urged by Gamaliel, his onetime mentor (Acts 5: 34–39); indeed he tells the Galatians that he *excessively persecuted the assembly of God, and ravaged it* (Galatians 1: 13) and that he was ahead of his contemporaries in his zeal for Judaism. Such vehemence made Jerusalem untenable for Christians. They either got out (except the apostles) or risked being dragged off to prison. Some were killed. Paul later told Agrippa that *when they were put to death I gave my vote* (Acts 26: 10) which suggests he may have been a member of the Sanhedrim.

... when the blood of thy witness Stephen was shed, I also myself was standing by and consenting, and kept the clothes of them who killed him.

Acts 22: 20

The persecution spread the Christian testimony throughout Judea and Samaria. Acts 8 tells how Philip evangelised successfully in Samaria, was used in the conversion of the Ethiopian eunuch in the Gaza desert, south west of Jerusalem, and then returned north, preaching as he went, until he reached Caesarea. Some disciples went further afield, to Phoenicia, Cyprus and Antioch (Acts 11: 19). The Jews must have received such reports with consternation. The movement they had tried to eradicate was spreading! The polity of the Sanhedrim extended to Jews outside Jerusalem, with the tacit approval of Rome, so Saul, although a Pharisee, went to the Sadducee chief priests for authority to arrest Christians in Damascus, all differences suppressed in common animosity against the disciples. There was a considerable Jewish community in Damascus and evidently several synagogues (Acts 9: 2, 20). No doubt Saul wanted to stop Christian Jews who had fled Jerusalem from making converts there. When testifying before Agrippa Paul said he had persecuted the saints *to cities out of our own land*, (Acts 26: 11) so Damascus may not have been the only city to which his zeal took him. The *authority and power* (Acts 26: 12) from the chief priests was forthcoming, and Saul set out on his journey.

the apostles
There is no record that the apostles fulfilled the special commission given to them by Christ in resurrection to *Go... and make disciples of all the nations* (Matthew 28: 19), or to *Go into all the world, and preach the good tidings to all the creation.* (Mark 16: 15). Even when the persecution against Christians was raging they remained in Jerusalem (Acts 8: 1) rather than follow the injunction *But when they persecute you in this city, flee to the other* (Matthew 10: 23). In God's ways Paul, although not one of the twelve, was specially and extraordinarily raised up and commissioned to become apostle of nations (Romans 11: 13).

Saul's journey to Damascus

Damascus is probably the oldest continuously inhabited city in the world. It is first mentioned in Scripture in Genesis 15: 2 in connection with Eliezer, Abraham's steward, and features in archives dating from the third millennium BC. The city has been subjected to many rulers through the centuries, but after Western Syria was annexed by the Roman General, Pompey, in 64 BC Damascus was incorporated into the Decapolis, a league of ten cities. At the time of Saul's conversion it was apparently under the control of Aretas IV, King of the Nabataeans, possibly having been ceded to him by the Roman emperor, Caligula (see 2 Corinthians 11: 32).

Saul's company no doubt included levites, or Temple Guards, to arrest leading Damascus Christians, and bring them back as captives to Jerusalem. They would have carried chains or ropes to bind the Christians, and perhaps rods to effect Jewish scourgings. Their most likely route

A distant view of Damascus, with a camel caravan in the foreground. Damascus is probably the oldest continuously inhabited city in the world, and in Paul's time it contained a large Jewish population.

JERUSALEM TO DAMASCUS

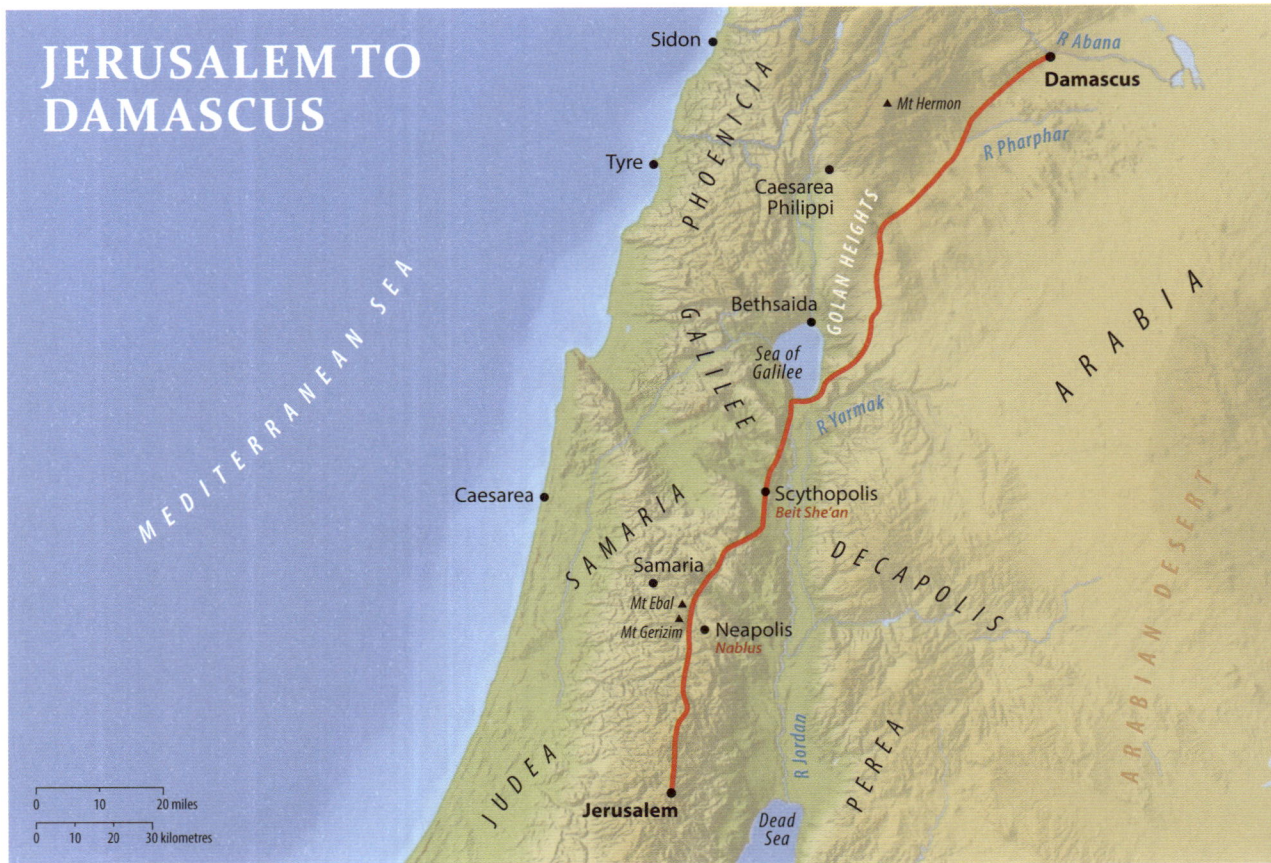

would have taken them northwards on the Roman road from Jerusalem to Neapolis, then past Samaria and down into the Jordan valley, probably crossing the river at Scythopolis. Next came the long grind up from the Sea of Galilee, about 700 feet (213 metres) below the Mediterranean, to Damascus, which was 2,264 feet (690 metres) above it – nearly 3,000 feet (914 metres) of ascent.

Jerusalem to Damascus

150 miles (241 km)

The whole journey would have taken six or eight days and Saul, freed for the moment from his frenetic activity in persecution, would have had time to reflect. The Lord would soon describe him as kicking against goads, which must surely refer to the inward struggle Saul was experiencing as he recalled Stephen's testimony and his prayer for his murderers even as they stoned him. This had given him enormous inspiration: he knew in his heart that Judaism could never produce anything like Stephen, and secretly longed to give up his hatred and rebellion against Christ. He showed excessive zeal in persecuting those he believed were betraying the religion of his fathers, but God had already begun a work in him which was impossible to resist. His

conversion must have come as an enormous relief in resolving the intense conflict raging within him.

Damascus is set on a plain below the Anti Lebanon mountains, watered by the Abana and Pharphar rivers (since renamed Barada and Awaj) which Naaman had preferred to the Jordan. The rivers made the area a fertile and verdant oasis, in contrast to the drab brown of the surrounding desert, and the white buildings of the city reflected the sun, inspiring the description *a diamond set in an emerald*.

Travellers would normally stop and rest in the merciless mid-day heat, but Saul's vehemence drove him on until he encountered a light from heaven which was brighter than the sun (Acts 26: 13). His conversion, which was to have such far reaching results, took place as he drew near to Damascus (Acts 9: 3; 22: 6), evidently close enough for him to be led into the city by the hand. Saul had intended to enter on a mission of vengeance, to persecute the assembly. In fact he was led through the city walls unable to see, his

This view looks south-west from the site of the Arab village of El-Manshiya. The deep valley between the hills is called Samech and drains into the Sea of Galilee, seen in the far centre background. Paul's route to Damascus would have crossed this terrain.

powerful will broken, but having had the overwhelming experience of a personal, corporeal appearing from the One he had been persecuting.

What an extraordinary event his conversion was! When Stephen was killed Saul's enmity against Christ was at its height, expressing, in an absolute way, the hatred against God which had been shown through the ages, from Cain onwards. Yet it was at this point the Lord intervened, to show that His grace was greater than the hatred and *surpassingly over-abounded with faith and love* (1 Timothy 1: 14).

And I said, What shall I do, Lord? And the Lord said to me, Rise up, and go to Damascus, and there it shall be told thee of all things which it is appointed thee to do.

Acts 22: 10

Something had started to work in Saul after the killing of Stephen and he was born anew before the Lord appeared to him. In the instant when Saul looked into the eyes of Jesus, and realised that the One whom he had persecuted was not against him, every atom of opposition in his being was obliterated. When he fell to the ground the power of Satan over him was broken forever. His surrender was complete and the authority of Christ over him was total from that point: he did not rise up until the Lord gave him direction. Saul was brought back to what Stephen represented, and would carry it forward in power for more than quarter of a century.

THE HIDDEN YEARS

6

Acts 9 and Galatians 1 tell us about Paul's movements after his conversion. However there is much we do not know about this period of the Apostle's life, before he is found at Antioch.

Arabia

Paul told the Galatians that immediately after his conversion he made his own decision to go to Arabia (Galatians 1: 17). This is not mentioned by Luke: the time in Arabia must be fitted between verses 19 and 20 of Acts 9. Arabia at that time designated the area to the east and south of Palestine, occupied by the Nabataeans, ruled by King Aretas IV, with the red sandstone city of Petra as its capital. Some think Damascus was included within its boundaries, in which case Paul may not have travelled far. However the scorching, barren environment was free of influences that would divert him from the deep exercise involved in making a complete break with Judaism, and a full transfer to Christianity. This was essential

Petra in Jordan (previously Arabia). Paul's time in Arabia may have been spent in this barren environment.

to preserve the integrity of what God had committed to him. Paul had been utterly steeped in Judaism, by genealogy, upbringing and training, and his complete renunciation of the entire corpus shows the immense depth of his conversion. The extended time in Arabia that followed was used to purge the last vestiges of Judaism from his being. The only thing he carried forward into Christianity was his knowledge of the Old Testament scriptures. Paul, the most brilliant scholar Judaism had ever produced, came under the complete management of Christ. His natural ability remained, but under a new Master.

Escape from Damascus

The reference to Aretas in 2 Corinthians 11: 32 is the only indication in ancient literature that Damascus was under Nabataean control at the time of Paul's conversion. The city was once in the Roman Province of Syria. After the death of Tiberius in 37 AD it was possibly ceded to the Arabians by Caligula. This was probably later than Saul's conversion.

King Aretas died in 40 AD, which gives promise of establishing a date for Paul's escape. The Emperor Trajan annexed the kingdom in 106 AD and turned it into the Province of *Arabia Pettraea*, but in Paul's time it was apparently a client kingdom of Rome. It looks as if Aretas had autonomy over Damascus, exercised through his ethnarch (governor), but possibly still under Rome's overall control.

From Galatians 1: 18 we learn that three years elapsed between Paul's conversion and his first visit to Jerusalem. This could mean three full years or, according to the Jewish way of reckoning, one full year and parts of two years. No doubt this time was spent in Arabia. After Paul returned to Damascus from Arabia his testimony confounded the Jews, who consulted to kill him. The ethnarch appointed by King Aretas co-operated with them, guarding the city gates to prevent Paul's escape, but the disciples saved his life by lowering him down through the wall, at night, in a basket. From the apostle's reference in 2 Corinthians 11: 33 he clearly found this a humiliating experience.

The ruins of a Roman arch in Damascus Old Town.

Paul's first visit to Jerusalem

What a change had come about in the apostle as he retraced the route used when he set out from Jerusalem for Damascus with letters from the high priest! He was now returning to Jerusalem as a penitent and broken believer, but nevertheless conscious of the great commission that had been entrusted to him. The grace that had met him filled his being and motivated his service for the rest of his life, so that he put far more zeal into Christianity than he had into Judaism.

Paul informs the Galatians that during his fifteen days in Jerusalem the only apostles he saw were Peter, and James the brother of the Lord (Galatians 1: 18, 19). He is very definite about this (verse 20) to emphasise that he did not receive his ministry from the apostles, although without doubt he would have absorbed from them all they could tell him about Christ. The account in the Acts, which is more generalised, records how Barnabas introduced him to the apostles, and related Paul's conversion to them (Acts 9: 26–30). His discussions with the Hellenists only ended in their trying to kill him and, as he recounts later, the Lord commanded him to get out of the city. This was a significant appearing, setting the direction of his service, that he was being sent to the nations afar off (Acts 22: 17–21). When Paul later recounted it to the Jews, on the steps of the Antonia fortress, they again tried to kill him: nothing had changed between his first and final visits to Jerusalem. After the attempt on Paul's life the brethren escorted him to Caesarea, a journey of about sixty-two miles (100 km) and sent him away to Tarsus (Acts 9: 30) so that he did not visit any other assemblies in Judea, and the brethren there did not know him by sight (Galatians 1: 22).

Caesarea was the home of Philip (Acts 8: 40, 21: 8), and of Cornelius (Acts 10). The city had been rebuilt in magnificent style by Herod the Great, and named in honour of the Roman emperor, Caesar Augustus. It had become the Roman metropolis of Judaea and official residence of the Herodian kings, and Roman Procurators, and was also a significant port. The simplest way of reaching Tarsus would have been by ship, although it is possible Paul could have followed the coastal road up to Antioch of Syria, through the Amanus Mountains and across the Cilician plain.

Paul in Syria and Cilicia

In Galatians 1: 21 Paul says he came into the regions of Syria and Cilicia. Fourteen years elapsed between his first visit to Jerusalem (Galatians 1: 18)

Damascus to Jerusalem
150 miles (241 km)

Caesarea to Tarsus
350 miles (563 km) by sea,
420 miles (676 km) by land

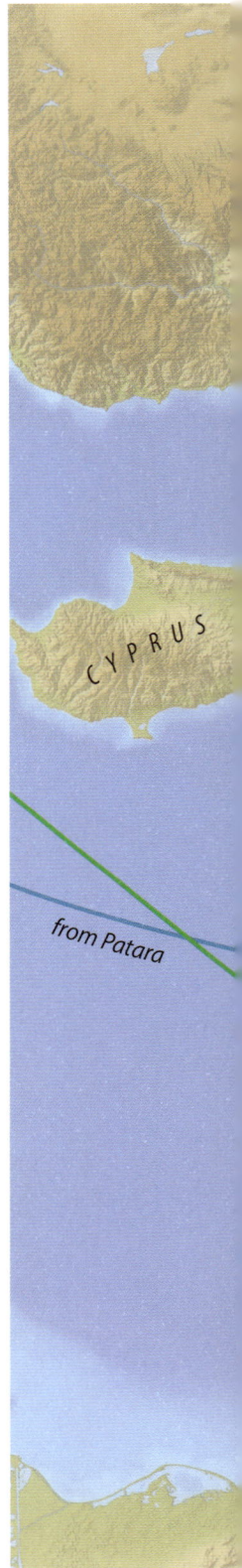

and his third visit (Galatians 2: 1, Acts 15). Even allowing several years for the period from when Paul first arrived in Antioch (Acts 11: 26) to his third visit to Jerusalem (Acts 15), this still leaves a number of years spent presumably in Syria and Cilicia, of which we have no knowledge.

Paul's list of his sufferings in 2 Corinthians 11 includes several more events than are recounted in the Acts. He was often in prison and was beaten on five occasions by the Jews, as well as being scourged three times, probably by the civil authorities. One of these was presumably the occasion at Philippi. In addition he suffered three shipwrecks and spent a night and a day in the ocean, no doubt after his ship broke up or sank. It is possible some of these sufferings took place in this early period. However this is not certain, since Luke is selective in what he includes in the Acts and is writing with a purpose, rather than to provide a detailed chronology of events. It is also important to note that the economy or administration given to Paul (see 1 Corinthians 3: 10; Ephesians 3: 1, 2; Colossians 1: 23–25), although it had always existed in the counsels of God, was only put into execution when he was commissioned at Antioch for his first western journey (Acts 13: 2).

Paul tells the Galatians that he was unknown personally to the assemblies in Judea, although they had heard about his conversion (Galatians 1: 22). This must have changed, however, since he tells Agrippa that he had announced repentance *to all the region of Judea* (Acts 26: 20). Since this service is not recorded in Acts it may have taken place before Paul was found in Antioch. Again, Acts 15: 41 refers to assemblies in Syria and Cilicia. It is possible some could have been established during this time, since Paul and Barnabas did not visit Cilicia on their first missionary journey.

... appointing to ministry him who before was a blasphemer and persecutor, and an insolent overbearing man...

1 Timothy 1: 13

Whatever the timescale of Paul's contacts with these assemblies there can be no doubt that he would have recounted his history and conversion to every gathering that he visited, and set himself to undo the damage he had caused. The apostle's brokenness and humility were such that no-one could doubt his sincerity, and the reality of the great change that had come about in him, as well as the divine authority governing his service as an elect vessel.

CYPRUS

from Patara

PAUL'S VISITS TO JERUSALEM

It appears from Scripture that Paul made five visits to Jerusalem after his conversion, and was arrested on his fifth visit there.

It is not straightforward to reconcile the accounts in the Acts and the epistle to the Galatians: they were written from different viewpoints, for different reasons and at different times. The summary below, however, follows the teaching of J.N. Darby (1800–1882).

First visit: from Galatians 1 we learn that Paul visited Jerusalem three years after his conversion following his time in Arabia. He went to make acquaintance with Peter, stayed with him fifteen days and saw no other apostles except James, brother of the Lord (Galatians 1: 16–19). He then went to Syria and Cilicia.

This is the visit referred to in Acts 9: 26. The account there omits the time spent in Arabia since the writer is concerned with establishing his place among Christians. At some stage, perhaps later, Barnabas introduced him to the apostles and related his conversion.

The appearing in the temple which Paul relates to the Jews in Acts 22: 17–21 evidently took place on this visit. Because of the attempt by Hellenists to kill him the brethren took him to Caesarea and sent him to Tarsus, which agrees with the reference in Galatians 1: 21 to Syria and Cilicia.

Second visit: Barnabas and Saul took the collection for Judea from Antioch to Jerusalem, Acts 11: 30. They brought John, surnamed Mark, back with them, Acts 12: 25.

Third visit: Paul and Barnabas went with others from Antioch to a conference at Jerusalem to agree the requirements for Gentile converts to be received into the assembly, as detailed in Acts 15. From Galatians 2: 1 we learn this took place fourteen years after his first visit, that he took Titus with him, and that he went up by revelation. Acts 15 gives the outward history whereas in Galatians 2 the apostle recounts the inward motives that governed him.

Fourth visit: Paul cut short his third western journey and declined to stay on at Ephesus so that he could be in Jerusalem *to keep the coming feast* – probably the Passover (Acts 18: 21). Luke's only comment on this visit is that he *saluted the assembly*.

Fifth visit: Paul went to Jerusalem on his final visit out of the conviction of his heart, knowing he was going into danger (Acts 21, 22). His arrest followed, and the end of his public ministry, according to the Acts. The attempts to kill him on his first and fifth visits showed that nothing had changed in Jerusalem during the intervening period.

Paul in Antioch and Jerusalem

Meanwhile the centurion Cornelius, and a number of gentiles, had received the word of God from Peter and been accepted by the assembly in Jerusalem. And in Antioch a large number of Greeks also believed and turned to the Lord after being spoken to by Cyprian and Cyrenian disciples who had left Jerusalem to escape the persecution. The assembly in Jerusalem, still assuming a metropolitan role, sent Barnabas to investigate. After encouraging the new converts, and no doubt feeling the need for help to consolidate the work, he went to Tarsus to look for Saul, found him and brought him back to Antioch (Acts 11: 20–26). He thus made way for a superior ability to come into the management. If the season permitted these journeys may have been by ship. The alternative route by land would have followed the coastal road north before crossing the Amanus mountains and traversing the Cilician plain.

The famine predicted by Agabus (Acts 11: 28) came to pass in the reign of Claudius Caesar who was emperor 41–54 AD. A famine in 45 AD particularly affected Judea and Syria, according to Josephus. Financial support from the Gentile church for the poor brethren in Jerusalem was to become a feature of Paul's administration – see Romans 15: 25, 26; 1 Corinthians 16: 1; and 2 Corinthians 9. Barnabas and Saul took the collection to Jerusalem themselves – Saul's second visit since his conversion. They would have taken the coastal route through Syria and Phoenicia and on their return they brought back John, surnamed Mark, who was Barnabas's cousin. From Acts 12: 25 it looks as if they got back to Antioch soon after the death of Herod Agrippa, which was in 44 AD.

SECTION 3

THE THREE GREAT JOURNEYS

"TO THE NATIONS AFAR OFF"

7

Paul's first western journey

From chapter 13 of the Acts Luke's narrative is nearly all about Paul. It represents a significant break in the book. Up to that point, from what little we know, Paul's ministry had been in the Levant. Acts 13 begins the account of his three great journeys to the west. Antioch in Syria is the starting point for each of them.

The city was founded around 300 BC by Seleukus Nicator and became capital of the Seleucid kingdom. Pompey took it in 66 BC and made it the seat of administration for the province of Syria. In Paul's time it was probably the third largest city in the world, after Rome and Alexandria, with a population, according to Strabo (*Geography* 16.2.5) of around three hundred thousand. Notorious for its profligacy, Antioch was an important political and commercial centre and headquarters of the Roman garrison in Syria. The population included Greeks, Syrians and Jews.

Luke goes into some detail about the formation of the assembly in Antioch. Originally disciples had fled there to escape the persecution in Jerusalem. Then Cyprians and Cyrenians started to preach to the Greeks, with immediate results: *a great number believed and turned to the Lord* (Acts 11: 21). This development did not escape the notice of the assembly in Jerusalem and Barnabas was sent out to consolidate the work, who sought out Saul at Tarsus, and brought him to Antioch.

Antioch in Syria, the city from which Barnabas and Saul were sent forth by the Holy Spirit on the first western journey (Acts 13: 4).

However Acts 12 and 13 show further development. The assembly in Antioch was now functioning with its own administration. A collection was arranged for the brethren in Judea. And a direct communication was received from the Holy Spirit (Acts 13: 2) which resulted in Barnabas and Saul being sent out, having the support of the brethren in the place.

It was now over a decade since Paul's conversion. All his experience and training under God were co-ordinated to serve his Master in the three great missionary journeys which he undertook, and which had such far reaching effects for humanity.

The voyage to Cyprus

Barnabas and Saul, with John Mark as their attendant, embarked at Seleucia Pieria, the commercial and naval port for Antioch, and the artery for the city's trade and expansion. It lay close to the mouth of the Orontes river, and although this was navigable as far as Antioch the twists and turns made the journey between the two centres by ship about 41 miles (66 km) whereas by land it was less than half that distance. The account in Acts says *went down to Seleucia* so it seems likely that Paul and his companions would have reached the port by road.

Seleucia to Salamis

135 miles (217 km)

A sea voyage from Seleucia direct to Salamis was only possible in the spring. In summer and autumn prevailing winds were from the west so that ships embarking from the Syrian coast could only reach northern harbours in Cyprus, and there was no sea travel in winter. So spring was the probable season for the start of Paul's journey.

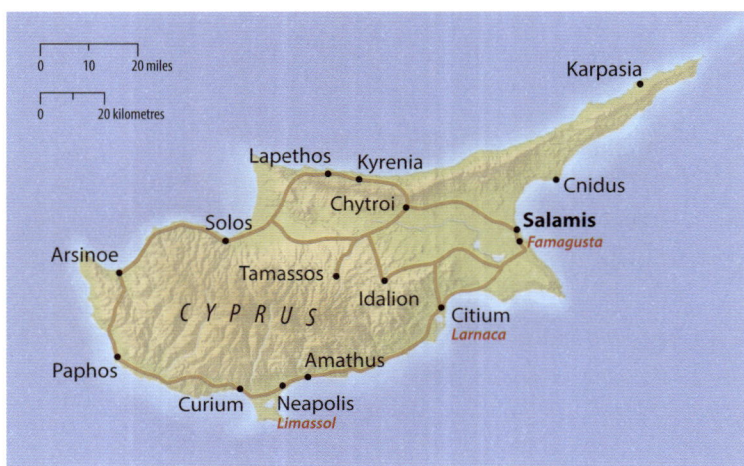

The travellers would have had no difficulty in finding a ship bound for Cyprus. Salamis was about 135 miles (217 km) from Seleucia, so assuming a favourable wind the voyage might have taken around 24 hours. We are not told of any plan Paul may have had for the whole journey. However Cyprus was a convenient starting point as a stepping stone to Asia, Jewish communities were well established there, and the island was the home of Barnabas. In addition some Cyprians, according to Acts 11: 20, were already Christians.

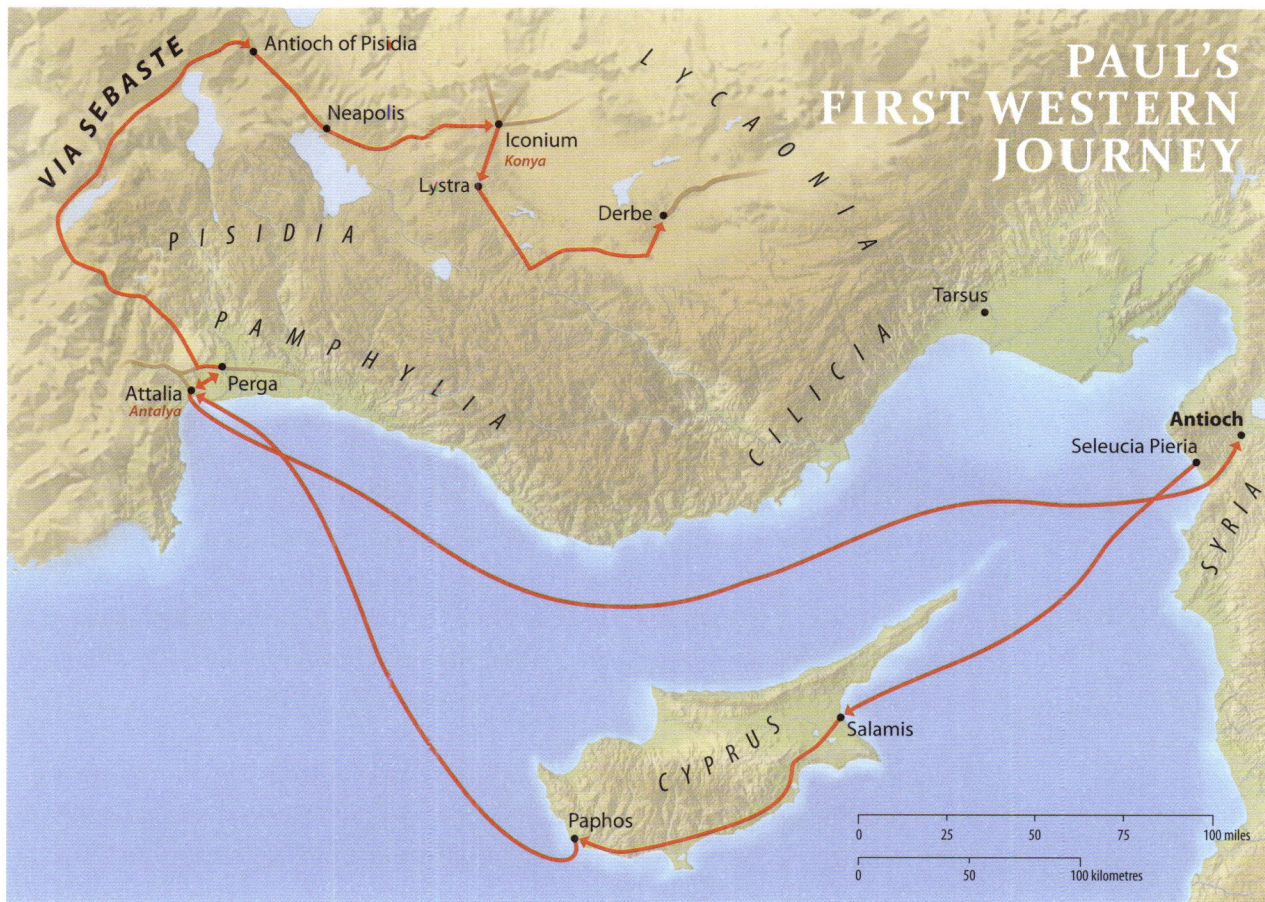

PAUL'S FIRST WESTERN JOURNEY

The island had been annexed by the Romans in 57 BC, and made a separate province in 27 BC. In 22 BC Augustus transferred it to the control of the Roman senate, so from then on it was administered by a proconsul, like other senatorial provinces.

Salamis, near modern Famagusta, was the island's main commercial centre during the Roman period. There were a number of synagogues, according to Acts 13: 5. The Jews would be attracted by the productivity of the island and its opportunities for trade, which included copper mining.

It is likely the apostle and his companions would have travelled by road along the south coast passing through the cities of Citium, Amathus and Curium before reaching Paphos. This city was known for its licentiousness, and worship of Aphrodite, Greek goddess of love and beauty, pervaded the culture. It was here that Paul confronted Elymas the magician, a renegade Jew who was breaking the Jewish law by dabbling in magic (see Deuteronomy 18: 10–14).

'to Jew first'

Paul started his service by preaching to the Jews. Although apostle to the Gentiles he was always faithful to the principle *to Jew first and to Greek* (Romans 1: 16).

Salamis to Paphos

115 miles (185 km)

Paphos harbour, where Paul and his company embarked for Perga of Pamphylia (Acts 13: 13).

The result was the conviction of Sergius Paulus, the Roman proconsul, and this conversion of a Gentile who had no connection with the synagogue was a significant confirmation of Paul's commission to evangelise the nations (Acts 22: 21).

From this point in the narrative Luke uses only the apostle's Roman name, *Paul*. He may have already possessed this name, possibly as the *cognomen* of his Roman name, but it is more likely that the apostle adopted it as the Roman or Gentile version of his Jewish name *Saul*. He is not called Saul again in the Acts from this point, nor does he use the name in any of his epistles. The Saul of the past, who had persecuted Christians, was now Paul, the apostle of the nations.

There was another significant change: the apostle now clearly took the lead, and this is reflected in Luke's designation *Paul and Barnabas*, instead of the other way round. The travellers sailed from the harbour at Paphos, a short distance from the town.

'Saul, who also is Paul' (Acts 13: 9)
Most Roman males had three names, such as *Marcus Licinius Crassus*, or *Gaius Julius Caesar*.

The first name, the *praenomen* was a personal or given name, to distinguish different family members, and used primarily within the family. Roman *praenomens* were generally chosen from a relatively small selection and included Decimus, Gaius, Publius and Tertius (the third).

The middle name, the *nomen* or *gentilicium* was a family name, indicating which gens a Roman belonged to, a gens being a loose collection of families, like a clan.

The last name, the *cognomen* was the name of the family line within the gens, and distinguished different persons in the same gens. It was a family name, shared by a group of blood relatives.

The cities of the plateau

We are not told what governed the decision to go to Pamphylia which at that time was an imperial province, *Lycia et Pamphylia*, bounded by the imperial Provinces of Cilicia to the east, Galatia to the north and the senatorial Province of Asia to the west. However the cities visited by Paul on this first journey were important centres on the great land route from Rome to Syria, a vital conduit for supplies from the east, but which would also serve for the spread of the gospel. Cities on this thoroughfare, from east to west, included the coastal cities of Caesarea, Antioch in Syria and Tarsus; then the cities of the Taurus plateau, Derbe, Iconium, Antioch of Pisidia, Apamea and Laodicea; and the Aegean ports of Ephesus, Corinth and Athens. Another benefit for Paul was that the cities of Lycaonia, Pamphylia and Phrygia were well connected by the *Via Sebaste*. This network of roads was built by the emperor, Augustus, in 6 BC to connect the military colonies that had been established to control the wild tribes of the Taurus region.

PAUL'S CITIES

York, England, was a Roman colony. The picture shows the remains of the Roman city wall in the foreground.

Before considering Paul's great journeys it is helpful to understand the character of the cities he visited. Although geographically diverse, many shared common features. Typically they had formed as settlements, some ancient. After Alexander's conquests they had become Hellenised, taking on features of Greek culture such as athletics, games, drama and music, and developed into civil communities with a body of free citizens. Later they came under the dominion of Rome. And some also had Jewish communities. So cities were often characterised by elements of Greek, Roman and Jewish culture, and in some cases descendants of the original settlers also were present.

The Romans were able to administer their vast empire using a surprisingly small number of State officials by delegating authority to local and provincial governments. Cities were given a status, which could be changed in the course of events. The most prestigious were *coloniae* – colonies. These were originally Roman outposts established in conquered territory, with citizens, often veteran soldiers, relocated from Rome. They were given land to farm which had been taken or bought from the native population. Colonies were modelled on the Roman constitution and, like most Mediterranean cities, were governed by an Assembly, a Council and Magistrates (called *duumviri*, or *prcetors*). The colonists had full Roman citizenship and the colonies were extensions of Rome itself, even if far afield, such as York *Eboracum* in England, and Lyon *Lugdunum* in France. Six of Paul's cities were colonies: Antioch of Pisidia, Iconium, Lystra, Troas, Philippi and Corinth.

Other classifications of Roman cities included free cities, *civitates liberae*, such as Thessalonica, Athens and Antioch in Syria. They were virtually self governing and were exempted from occupation by a Roman carrison. And the largest group was ordinary tributary cities, *civitates stipendariae*, in which were found Salamis in Cyprus, Derbe, Perga, Berea, and Ephesus. The writer of the Acts was clearly well acquainted with the different statuses of Roman cities, and accurately records their characteristics where this is relevant to his narrative.

Roman provinces *provinciae* were the largest administrative and territorial units, often with vaguely defined borders, and the number of provinces changed as more territories were conquered. For example the district of Pamphylia, which Paul visited on his first western journey, was taken from the province of Galatia in 43 AD and linked with Lycia to form a new province, Lycia-Pamphylia. Provinces where Roman legions were stationed had governors under the emperor and were known as imperial provinces. But most were senatorial provinces, governed by proconsuls who were usually former *praetors*. Paul visited at least eight different provinces in the course of his service.

Mark abandons Paul

As the ship approached the Bay of Attalia from the south-east the sailors would have seen Perga, capital of the Pamphylia region, at the forefront of a great plain. Behind the city the snow capped Taurus mountains rose in a majestic backdrop, a formidable massif with many peaks over 10,000 feet (3,000 metres). Crossing such a barrier on foot or on asses was no light matter, but there was no alternative route from the coastal plain to the cities of the plateau.

... and John separated from them and returned to Jerusalem.

Acts 13: 13

Perga was the terminus of the *Via Sebaste* which gave access to the Anatolian plateau. When they landed there, Mark left Paul and Barnabas and returned to Jerusalem. Probably he boarded a ship bound for Caesarea. Luke gives no reason for his action, but Mark must have been tested by events not working out as he had anticipated. The journey had begun in Cyprus with Barnabas, his relative, at the forefront, but in dealing with Elymas Paul had come forward in evident power, taking the lead. Now he was proposing to press on and cross these awesome mountains into unknown territory.

It was a retrograde step for Mark to leave Paul, and return to the familiarity of Jerusalem, where his natural family lived (Acts 12: 12). Paul later referred to him as having *abandoned them* (Acts 15: 38). Painful years of exercise were involved before he was fully recovered to Paul, and serviceable to him for ministry (2 Timothy 4: 11).

Over the mountains

Paul and Barnabas do not appear to have stayed in Perga, which was 9 miles (14 km) east of modern Antalya, but pressed on to Antioch of Pisidia. By May the snows blocking the mountain passes would have dispersed, and there would have been a general movement out of the city to escape from the heat of the coastal plain to the cooler mountain slopes. If Paul left Seleucia in early spring – the seas being technically open for travel from March – his arrival at Perga could well have coincided with this exodus of the people with their herds.

The journey to Antioch of Pisidia involved over 4,000 feet (1,220 m) of ascent. The travellers most likely went west across the plain on the *Via Sebaste* to Lyrba, then began the traverse of the mighty Taurus range, climbing up through the Klimax pass. Initially the road wound upwards through thickets of pomegranates and oleanders, and then through forests of oak, pine and cedar. The final stage was up jagged mountain passes before

emerging to the interior plateau. A milestone still stands at the summit of the pass giving a distance of 139 Roman miles to Antioch of Pisidia. An alternative route from Perga to Antioch of Pisidia was shorter and more direct but involved steep ascents through the ravines of the Taurus mountains. Paul and Barnabas may have used this other route for descent, on their return to Perga, Acts 14: 25.

These routes involved some danger, and help to explain Paul's words to the Corinthians *in perils of rivers, in perils of robbers* (2 Corinthians 11: 26). The mountainous area of Pisidia is networked with watercourses which are subject to sudden and violent changes so that travellers, if they escape being swept away, may be cut off with little warning. And on the bleak steppes of the plateau sudden rainfall can transform the terrain into a sea of mud making progress impossible. Although the *Pax Romana* under Augustus had greatly improved security for travellers, and the major roads were patrolled, lawless bands of robbers still operated from the security of the mountains, and were a constant threat to the unwary.

This is the view that Paul and his companions would have had as they approached the Bay of Attalia, after sailing from Paphos. Although beautiful to look at, the mighty Taurus Mountains were a formidable and dangerous barrier which had to be crossed to reach the cities of the plateau. As soon as they landed in Pamphylia, Mark abandoned Paul and Barnabas and returned to Jerusalem (Acts 13: 13).

Paphos to Antioch of Pisidia

340 miles (547 km)

Paul and Barnabas must have missed the help of their late companion on this hazardous route but after traversing the uplands arrived at Antioch of Pisidia, a major Roman colony whose ruins lie about 1 mile (1.6 km) north of modern Yalvaç on the southern foothills of the Sultan mountains, about 4,055 feet (1,236 metres) above sea level. It was the head of the *Via Sebaste*, with branches to Iconium and Lystra, with a population made up of native Galatians, Phrygians, Roman military veterans, Jews and others.

Ruins of Antioch of Pisidia (near modern Yalvac, Turkey).

Antioch and Iconium

Luke has given a full report of Paul's address at Antioch of Pisidia, which no doubt was typical of many others to follow. The apostle's consistent approach was to the Jews first, right up to their rejection in Acts 28. He used events and Scriptures from the Old Testament not only to reason that the incoming of Jesus was the fulfilment of prophecy as to a Saviour, but also to proclaim justification, by virtue of the death and burial of Christ, to *every one that believes* (Acts 13: 39). His words were received with great interest, but on the following Sabbath unbelieving Jews vehemently opposed his teachings and enlisted influential Gentiles against Paul and Barnabas to force them out of the city.

Jewish opposition

The reaction to Paul's preaching at Antioch of Pisidia was repeated in many cities where the apostle served. Although they were approached first, the Jews as a body invariably came out in opposition against the gospel, although individuals believed, but many Gentile worshippers came into blessing. It was a significant moment when Paul declared *lo, we turn to the nations* in fulfilment of Isaiah 49: 6.

PAUL'S CONVERTS

Although Paul's mission was to the Gentiles, he did not fail to show respect for God's chosen people. In most cases the synagogue was the starting point for his preaching. Synagogues were attended by interested Gentiles, as well as Jews. A few of these, known as *proselytes of the sanctuary*, had been formally received into Judaism, the men having been circumcised. But most were Gentiles, the men not having been circumcised, but preferring Jewish worship to the degradation of idolatry. These provided fertile ground for a gospel which offered reconciliation to God and righteousness by faith, without the demands of male circumcision, and keeping the law of Moses. Such were known as *proselytes of the gate, worshipping proselytes, worshippers* or *God-fearers* and there are many references in the Acts to this numerous class of persons, which included Lydia, Acts 16: 14. See also Acts 13: 16, 43, 50; 17: 4, 17; and 18: 7. Their conversion to Christianity was resented by the Jews.

Far from restricting the servants, opposition had the effect of spreading the testimony. Paul and Barnabas moved on to Iconium (modern Konya), a straightforward journey along the *Via Sebaste*. Iconium was one of the world's oldest cities. Its position at the western edge of the great Anatolian plateau at a height of 3,600 feet (1,100 metres) was strategic because here the *Via Sebaste* joined the main highway which linked Asia Minor with the east. At this time Iconium consisted of a Hellenised *polis* and a prosperous Roman colony, established by Augustus, on the same site. Once again Paul's speaking produced results, and once again opposition instigated by unbelieving Jews forced Paul and Barnabas to leave the city for the region of Lycaonia. The reference to *surrounding country* in Acts 14: 6 is the only occasion in Acts where Paul is found ministering outside cities or towns.

Antioch in
Pisidia to
Iconium

100 miles (161 km)

apostles
Luke calls Paul and Barnabas *apostles* in Acts 14: 4 and 14. Elsewhere in the Acts he reserves this designation for the Twelve.

Several of the cities visited by Paul on his first western journey were situated on the Anatolian plateau, the great central plain to the north of the Taurus mountains.

The apostle survives stoning

Lystra and Derbe lay south east of Iconium on the route through the Cilician Gates to Tarsus and Syria. Lystra, having strategic importance, was made a Roman colony by Augustus in 6 BC. There is no mention of a synagogue, although Acts 16: 3 indicates a Jewish population in the area, and the crowds evidently spoke in Lycaonian (Acts 14: 11) which is evidence that the original native tongues co-existed with Greek in cities that had become Hellenised. After healing the man who had never walked, Paul confronted superstition and mythology when the crowds credited the apostle and his companion with being the heathen deities who patronised their locality: Barnabas they designated as Jupiter (Zeus), king and ruler of the Olympian gods, and Paul as Mercury (Hermes), their messenger, renowned for his eloquence. Historians have speculated from this that Barnabas may have been more imposing in stature than Paul, whose Roman name means *little* and whose

*Iconium
to Lystra*

21 miles (34 km)

'disciples' (Acts 14: 20)
Who were the *disciples* who cared for Paul when he was stoned at Lystra? Had the city already been evangelised? Or were these persons new converts? Paul and Barnabas had stayed a *good while* at Iconium, so it may be disciples from that city had followed him to Lystra, which was only 21 miles (34 km) away. It should be remembered that Acts is a summary of key events, and the timescale is not always given. We do not know how long Paul and Barnabas stayed in the cities of the plain.

physical presence was evidently despised by the Corinthians (2 Corinthians 10: 10). After being restrained from offering sacrifices to Paul and Barnabas the fickle crowd was incited by Jews from Antioch and Iconium to stone Paul. This was a seditious action following no legal process, although it took place within the city. The Jews then drew Paul out of Lystra, presumably following their procedure for dealing with the body of a blasphemer, but the apostle, having been encircled by the disciples, rose up undaunted and re-entered the city. The apostle's reference in 2 Corinthians 12: 2–4 no doubt relates to his experience at this time. According to 2 Corinthians 11: 25 this is the only occasion when Paul was stoned – and to survive a Jewish stoning was indeed rare, since it was intended to kill.

Timothy may have met Paul, or heard him speak, during the apostle's visit to the region, or Paul and Barnabas may even have been accommodated in his house. When Timothy came to light during Paul's second visit to Lystra, Acts 16: 1, he was already a disciple, and the reference in 2 Timothy 3: 11 shows that Timothy knew all about Paul's sufferings at Antioch, Iconium and Lystra. We are not told if he was an eyewitness or heard of them from others.

Back to Antioch

Return to Antioch in Syria
720 miles (1,159 km) from Derbe

Total journey
around 1550 miles (2494 km)

It shows the apostle's extraordinary courage and resilience that the next day after his ordeal he was able to set out for the military outpost of Derbe which was about 85 miles (137 km) from Lystra. After making many disciples there he and Barnabas retraced their steps to Lystra, Iconium and Antioch of Pisidia, strengthening the disciples and choosing elders to exercise care in each nascent assembly. It shows Paul's selflessness that he was prepared to return to these places where he had been so badly treated. They again passed through Perga, on this occasion speaking the word before embarking from Attalia to Antioch in Syria, a voyage of 350 miles (563 km).

So Paul and Barnabas returned from their eventful journey to be welcomed by the assembly in Antioch (Acts 14: 26–28). They had travelled some 1,550 miles (2,494 km). Paul's distinctive leadership had become manifest. His trusted attendant had deserted them. And the apostle had suffered intense opposition from unbelieving Jews, been attacked by pagans and brought to the point of death by stoning. Nevertheless the gospel had been received in the hearts of many disciples, and a number of assemblies established, which were functioning under the care of elders.

NEW WINE AND OLD SKINS

8

Paul's third visit to Jerusalem

The conference described in Acts 15, attended by Paul and Barnabas, was an attempt to settle opposing views as to what demands should be made of Gentile converts. It was held at Jerusalem. The believers there had reformed after the persecution which followed Stephen's death, and had survived Herod's antagonism. There had also been new converts, including Pharisees (Acts 15: 5). This seems to be where the trouble originated.

These Jewish believers saw Christianity as a new movement which could be included within Judaism. They recognised Jesus as Messiah, but would not set aside the law of Moses. So they were only willing to admit Gentiles if they submitted to being circumcised, and made a commitment to keep the law.

Although they had nominally accepted Jesus as their Messiah they failed to accept that the authority of the Law of Moses over the conscience had been terminated at the cross and superseded by Christian grace. They were opposing Christianity from within as surely as their unbelieving brethren were opposing it from without.

Paul, by contrast, was preaching remission of sins through Jesus, involving a wider justification than the law could provide, to be obtained by believing (Acts 13: 39). Gentiles who embraced his glad tidings were being received into the Church, evidently in considerable numbers.

The question affected the very foundation of Christianity: to insist on circumcision meant being governed by the law, at the expense of grace. This affected the rights of God and was a denial of the sinful condition of man, which only grace could meet.

The bringing in of Cornelius and his house had set a precedent which, had it been followed, would have resolved the difficulty. The signs and the reception of the Holy Spirit at that time had shown beyond all doubt that God was in the movement. But the power of Judaism, concentrated in Jerusalem, was immense, and the disciples there were attempting to fulfil the Jewish law and temple worship as well as maintaining Christian fellowship, which was still the case at Paul's fifth and final visit (Acts 21: 20). The epistle to the Hebrews, some years later, was a final appeal to leave the Jewish camp, before the Roman invasion obliterated the testimony in Jerusalem forever.

Antioch to Jerusalem
360 miles (579 km)

It was repugnant to an unenlightened Jew, schooled from infancy to observe the law, and brought up in strict separation from Gentiles, never eating with them, to have fellowship with converts from a culture associated in their eyes with profligacy and idolatry. Only a new life in Christ could overcome the deep prejudice. Otherwise it was impossible for the new wine to be accommodated in the old skin.

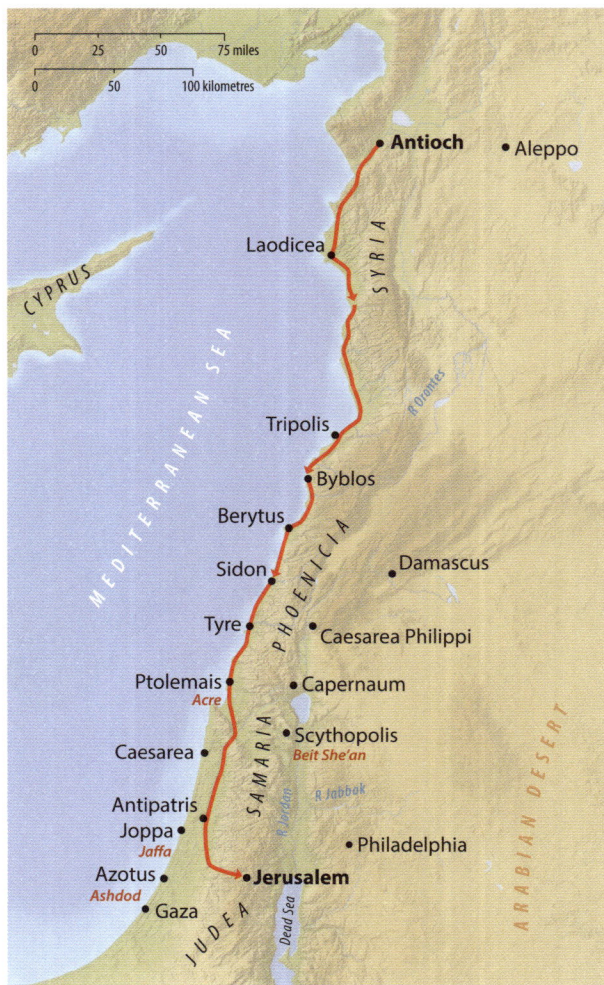

"False brethren"

Antioch was evidently a mixed assembly, with Jews and Gentiles working out the truth together. Unity was threatened when some came from Judea and asserted that salvation depended on circumcision (Acts 15: 1). It seems they used the names of the apostles, without any authority, to justify this view (Acts 15: 24). Luke describes them as *certain persons*. Paul bluntly calls them *false brethren* (Galatians 2: 4). Discussion having failed to resolve the issue, Paul, Barnabas and others were delegated to go to Jerusalem and put the question to the apostles and elders. Luke gives the outward history, but Paul later tells the Galatians that he went up to Jerusalem according to revelation (2: 2) and that he took Titus with him. It was a bold strategy to take an uncircumcised Greek into the centre of Judaism, but Titus demonstrated a genuine work of God. Circumcision would have added nothing to him. Barnabas, by contrast, was a Jew, a Levite, and well known to the apostles.

From Antioch the party would have taken the road for Syrian Laodicea, and then followed the road that hugged the Phoenician coast passing

Tripolis, Berytus, Sidon and Tyre before turning south-east through Samaria, evangelised by Philip, to Jerusalem. They had contact with assemblies on the way and accounts of the conversion of Gentiles were received with great joy. Phoenicia and Samaria are mentioned in Acts 15: 3 but not Judea. The whole journey might well have taken three weeks.

The Jerusalem conference

Paul came under attack as soon as he arrived at Jerusalem, with the Pharisees stridently insisting that Gentile converts should be circumcised and keep the Law of Moses. It appears from Galatians 2: 1–10 that Paul had a private meeting with James, Cephas and John, and told them about the gospel he preached to the Gentiles. Cephas and John were leading apostles and James, although not one of the twelve, had also seen the Lord and took a lead in the Jerusalem assembly. Paul was prepared, it appears, to submit his service to their judgement, but the result was clear: they were convinced by the irrefutable evidence that Paul had received a direct commission, independent of their own. Had the meeting been in earlier years Paul would not have been able to point to the results of his ministry. It was settled that he should continue with his mission to the nations, while they went to the circumcision. There was only one *caveat* – that Paul should remember the impoverished saints in Jerusalem and Judea. This is the only record of a meeting between Paul and John. And Acts 15 is the last mention of Peter in the Acts.

The public meeting followed. After much discussion had been allowed Peter rose and recounted how he had been used to bring in Cornelius, who had been received without any differences being made. He asked why they should tempt God *by putting a yoke upon the neck of the disciples, which neither our fathers nor we have been able to bear?* (Acts 15: 10). Barnabas and Paul were heard next, in respectful silence. They avoided controversy but simply related the works of power which had taken place among the Gentiles. James then made a conclusive speech, arguing from Amos (quoting from the Septuagint) that the incoming of the Gentiles was the fulfilment of prophecy, and that only four stipulations should be laid on Gentile converts. These were to abstain from pollution of idols, from fornication, from what is strangled and from blood.

These are described in the subsequent letter as *necessary things*. It was now required the Gentiles should renounce these practices, common among

The Old City, Jerusalem.

them, in the interest of maintaining unity. In fact the strictures originated before the law. Idolatry was an affront to God's authority; respect for life – the blood – as belonging to God had been laid on Noah; and marriage had been divinely instituted in Paradise. The injunctions relate to what is proper and orderly in relations between God and man.

Barnabas and Paul
The letter from Jerusalem described Barnabas and Paul as *men who have given up their lives for the name of our Lord Jesus Christ* (Acts 15: 26).

The letter was addressed only to Gentile believers at Antioch, in Syria and Cilicia. This is the first Scriptural mention of assemblies in Syria and Cilicia and we do not know how they originated. The conference did not assume universal authority. It was a meeting of the assembly in Jerusalem to respond to a delegation from the assembly at Antioch. The assembly did not vote, but all consented to the decision. It appears that the influence of James carried the day: he was the brother of the Lord, said to have been converted at the resurrection, and renowned for his piety and devotion.

The return to Antioch

Judas called Barsabas, and Silas, returned to Antioch with Paul and Barnabas as directed. They complemented the letter with their own testimony, which was received with rejoicing. In due course Judas returned to Jerusalem. Silas, however, seems to have remained in Antioch, according to the Authorised Version, which says as much in Acts 15: 34. Although this verse has been omitted from J.N. Darby's translations, as having been added at a later stage, what it said was no doubt correct. Silas wanted to stay with Paul. As J.N. Darby put it, *Silas... had preferred the work to Jerusalem instead of Jerusalem to the work* (Synopsis, volume 4, page 42). No doubt this helped to qualify him to be included with Paul on his second great journey.

The conference at Jerusalem averted a division which could have been fatal to the progress of Christianity. A resolution made at Antioch would not have carried the same authority. The settlement also left Paul free to pursue his own ministry, with the sanction of the apostles. He had received nothing from those prominent at Jerusalem and the leading apostles could not but recognise his credentials, and accept that he had been given a commission directly from Christ.

However the Judaisers in Jerusalem were unrepentant. During the rest of Paul's ministry they made systematic attempts to undermine the assemblies he had established – a heartbreaking experience for the apostle, his letter to the Galatians expressing how strongly he felt it.

9

THE GOSPEL REACHES EUROPE

... so that I, from Jerusalem, and in a circuit round to Illyricum, have fully preached the glad tidings of the Christ...

Romans 15: 19

The public ministry of Paul among the Gentiles, in his second and third missionary journeys, is recorded in Acts 15: 36 to 21: 15. This was a unique period in the development of Christianity when the apostle, under the direct commission of Christ, fulfilled his service in a great sweep of territory from Jerusalem as far as the Adriatic. The labours of this one man, undeterred by suffering, hardship or opposition, established a foothold of Christianity in Europe and thereby changed the history of the world. Although Paul had valued fellow workers he was the indisputable leader, giving impetus and direction to the movement.

Paul's second western journey – part one

Paul's second missionary journey involved a round trip of over 3,000 miles (4,828 km) as a result of which the Christian testimony was extended westwards into Europe. A number of new assemblies were established, and existing assemblies were confirmed. Copies of the decrees given at the Jerusalem conference were left with some assemblies as the means to refute any Judaisers who still insisted on Gentile circumcision.

Disagreement with Barnabas

Paul refused to agree to Barnabas's proposal that Mark should accompany them, on the grounds that he had previously abandoned them (Acts 13: 13). This led to a separation between these two valuable servants. Barnabas took Mark, his relative, and sailed for Cyprus, his native country. Paul, who had sacrificed all natural and national considerations for the sake of the work, chose Silas who had already shown his enthusiasm for Paul and the work at Antioch by staying there instead of returning to Jerusalem. Like Barnabas, he had been present at the Jerusalem conference so could bear first hand witness to the result. Acts 16: 37 suggests he also possessed Roman citizenship. They set out, having been committed by the brethren to the grace of God.

The route across the Taurus Mountains was through the Cilician Gates, a narrow pass 3,445 feet (1,050 metres) above sea level.

Across the mountains

Their route would have led northward, crossing the Amanus Mountains by the Syrian Gates (or Beilan Pass) a long valley about 2,165 feet (660 metres) above the Mediterranean, before descending to the coastal plain of Cilicia. We do not know how the assemblies in Cilicia began, nor do we know what cities the servants visited. If they followed the Roman roads these would have included Alexandria and Issus, on the western side of the Amanus range, and Mopsouhestia, Adana and Tarsus on the Cilician coastal plain.

Their route across the Taurus Mountains, the great barrier between Cilicia and Lycaonia, would have been through the Cilician Gates, a narrow river gorge with a southern entrance just 27 miles (43 km) north of Tarsus. The city's strategic importance was largely by virtue of its location on the trade route between Asia and the west. In ancient times the narrow walls of the pass had echoed the tramp of armies as leaders of the Persian and Greek empires – Xerxes, Cyrus the Younger, Xenophon and Alexander the Great – mobilised their troops for conquest. Now Paul and Silas, outwardly insignificant, were using the pass on a journey for spiritual conquest which would have infinitely greater results for humanity. Their route took them on to the *Via Tauri*, then westward across the plateau to Derbe, the furthest point visited on Paul's first journey. The distance from Antioch in Syria to Derbe by this route was about 255 miles (410 km). And it was here that Timotheus came to light.

Timotheus

Timothy may well have heard Paul, or had contact with him, at his first visit. He certainly knew about the apostle's sufferings in Iconium and Lystra (2 Timothy 3: 11). On one of these visits Paul had laid his hands on him, thereby conferring the gift of the Spirit (2 Timothy 1: 6), and this was repeated by the elderhood (1 Timothy 4: 14), a symbolic action to confirm a person had been selected for service. Timothy was also the subject of prophecy, and well reported of in the district. Paul's action in circumcising him was strategic, to pre-empt opposition. It was not a requirement of Jewish law, unless he had become a proselyte, but went some way to remove the reproach of mixed parentage and to forestall Jewish prejudice, so that Timothy would not be handicapped in the Lord's work. The marriage of Timotheus's Jewish mother was unclean according to the law, and would have rendered him also unclean and deprived him of his Jewish rights. It also provides an example of Paul's strategy to gain the most possible, which he outlined to the Corinthians: *And I became to the Jews as a Jew, in order that I might gain the Jews* (1 Corinthians 9: 20). By contrast the apostle had taken Titus, a Greek, into the centre of Jewish opposition at Jerusalem (Galatians 2: 3), refusing demands that he should be circumcised.

Phrygia and Galatia

After passing through Phrygia, which Paul had already visited on his first western journey, he and his company struck north, entering the province of Galatia for the first time. This was new territory.

Galatia took its name from the Gauls, the same people ethnically as the Celts of Britain and France. They had migrated from central Europe in the fourth and third centuries BC, first settling in north central Asia Minor (modern Turkey) before King Nicomedes I gave them land on the Anatolian plateau in return for military help from Galatian mercenaries. They became organised in three tribes: in the west were the Tolistboboii, whose capital was Pressinus; in the east were the Trocmi, centred around Tavium; and between them were the Tectosages, with Ancyra (modern Ankara) as their principal city. Government was initially by a central council, with four tetrarchs from each tribe, then by three tribal kings, but in 54 BC Deiotarus gained power as the first Galatian king. The location of Galatia was strategic: it was traversed by the Persian Royal Road, rebuilt by Darius I in the fifth century BC, which ran 1,677 miles (2,699 km) from Sardis in Asia Minor to Susa in modern Iran.

In the late first century BC the Galatians allied themselves with the Romans as the influence of the empire spread eastward, and in 64 BC Pompey rewarded them by designating Galatia a client kingdom and expanding its borders to include territory to the south and east. Amyntas, the third Galatian king was later given part of Cilicia and regions of Pisidia and Isauria by Augustus in return for support in the battle of Actium in 31 BC, which meant his kingdom included a large part of southern Asia Minor that had never been ethnically Galatian. After Amyntas died in 25 BC Augustus made Galatia a Roman province, which bordered with the provinces of Bithynia

THE NORTH & SOUTH GALATIAN THEORIES

Until the nineteenth century the references to Paul's visits to Galatia in Acts 16: 6 and 18: 23 were taken to mean the ancient kingdom of Galatia, which was later incorporated into the Roman province of the same name. This was the view taken by patristic, medieval and Reformation commentators, and is reflected in the routes of Paul's journeys indicated in older biblical maps.

In the nineteenth century a number of distinguished Bible scholars began to promote what became known as the *South Galatian Theory*, the view that the Galatian references in Acts 16: 6 and 18: 23 referred to the Roman province, rather than the ancient kingdom, and that the Galatian assemblies were those founded by Paul on his first western journey, including Antioch of Pisidia, Iconium, Lystra and Derbe. These cities were included in the Roman province when it was created in 25 BC with the possible exception of Iconium.

This question has been the subject of debate between scholars with a number of arguments advanced for each viewpoint. However the south Galatian theory, as it is known, has gained support and now tends to be widely accepted, despite lack of conclusive evidence.

In this study the author follows the teaching of J.N. Darby (1800 –1882) who evidently supports the view that references to Galatia are to the ancient kingdom, rather than the Roman province:

> They execute then this mission in Phrygia, and in the regions of Galatia. He had already commenced in Phrygia on his first journey, but now he enters Galatia, a large province, for the first time. (*Collected Writings*, volume 25 pages 384–385)

This quotation refers to Paul's second western journey, Acts 16: 6, and if this was the first time Paul entered Galatia then clearly different territory was involved than that covered on his first western journey.

Also the apostle's words that he had preached the glad tidings *from Jerusalem, and in a circuit round to Illyricum* (Romans 15:19) seem more understandable if we regard his visit to the ancient kingdom of Galatia as completing the northeast segment of that circuit.

and Pontus in the north, Asia in the west, Lycia, Pamphylia and Cilicia in the south, and Cappadocia in the east.

The Celts – Gauls – were known to be fiery, impulsive and fickle and have been described as a race that *shook all empires but founded none*. Paul's heartfelt exclamation *O senseless Galatians* (Galatians 3: 1) was no doubt a reference to their ethnic characteristics, rather than their geographic boundaries. Throughout their changes of political fortune they retained their Celtic language.

We do not know which Galatian cities the apostle visited, or how long he stayed. It seems he was afflicted with illness or disability, and many have speculated whether this had to do with the *thorn for the flesh* mentioned in 2 Corinthians 12: 7, possibly affecting his eyes. The Galatians, instead of being repelled by his condition, treated him with spontaneous kindness and received him as a divine messenger (Galatians 4: 14).

Paul's letter is addressed to the assemblies of Galatia, so there must have been several gatherings and this is confirmed by 1 Corinthians 16: 1. They may have included Jews as well as Gauls, and not long after the apostle's service to them the Galatians evidently came under the influence of Judaisers who insisted on circumcision. Paul's letter, rebuking them for their fickleness, may have been written on his third western journey, after his second visit to Galatia. In his second letter to Timothy he tells him that Crescens has gone to Galatia (4: 10).

The route to Europe

The province of Asia, with its great cities of Ephesus, Smyrna and Sardis must have seemed a likely field after Galatia but the Holy Spirit directed otherwise. Nor were Paul and his companions allowed to go north, to the province of Bithynia. They therefore headed west, their route taking them across wild and broken terrain, passing through Mysia, the most northerly of the three territories of the province of Asia, the other two being Lydia and Caria. Probably they followed the river Rhyndakos, then went westwards through Phrygia, keeping south of the large lakes, and down the Aegean coast to Troas, at the mouth of Hellespont (the Dardanelles). Luke compresses considerable time and distance into verses 6 to 8 of Acts 16, perhaps due to lack of information or because the detail was not relevant to his discourse. From Galatia to Troas involved a journey of some 400 miles (644 km) which could have taken several weeks.

A well preserved Roman bridge over the Kocaçay River, a tributary of the Rhyndakos.

Troas was the chief city in north-west Asia Minor, made a Roman colony in the time of Augustus, and visited by Paul on three occasions. The name came from the *Troes*, an ancient people of Troad whose territory became part of Mysia. The city became the nodal point on a nexus of international routes, so was strategically placed to facilitate the spread of the gospel into Europe. It was at Troas that Paul had the vision which convinced them to go to Macedonia – a momentous decision for the future of Europe and indeed the entire western world! Luke seems to have joined the group at this point, judging by the change from 'they' to 'we' in the account (Acts 16: 10), and also by the hallmarks of an eyewitness in the subsequent narrative.

The apostle and his companions embarked and set sail on the blue waters of the Aegean Sea with a good following wind. This took them to the island of Samothracia, with its 5,285 foot (1,611 metres) high peak of Mount Fengari, where they moored for the night. The next day they arrived at Neapolis and took the road over the Symbolum mountain ridge, at a height of 1,600 feet (488 metres) before descending to Philippi, twelve miles (19 km) inland. The two day voyage shows the advantage of a favourable breeze: in Acts 20: 6 the same trip, in the opposite direction, took five days.

the 'We' passages in Acts
There are three sections where the narrative is in the first person *we*, instead of *they*, from which it is assumed Luke has joined the party and is writing as an eyewitness. These are 16: 10 to 17: 1; 20: 5 to 21: 18; and 27: 1 to the end of the book.

Antioch in Syria to Philippi

1,200 to 1,300 miles (1931 to 2092 km)

BLAC[K]

Byzantium
Istanbul

ILLYRICUM

THRACE

MACEDONIA

Dyrrachium
Durrës

Philippi

Neapolis
Kavala

Amphipolis

Apollonia

MYSIA

Thessalonica
Thessaloniki

Samothracia

Troy

Berea
Veria

Lemnos

Troas

Adramyttium

Assos

Pergamos
Pergamum

EPIRUS

Lesbos

Mitylene

Thyatira

Aegean Sea

ASIA

Philadelphia

Nicopolis

LYDIA

Chios

Smyrna

Delphi

Thebes

Ephesus

Magnesia

Corinth

Athens

Samos

CARIA

Patmos

Miletus

ACHAIA

Olympia

Cos

Sparta

Rhode[s]

Rhodes

CRETE

Fair Havens
Kali Limenes

PAUL'S SECOND WESTERN JOURNEY

0 — 50 — 100 miles
0 — 50 — 100 kilometres
– – – (route uncertain)

SEA

BITHYNIA

PONTUS

...caea

Tavium

Ancyra
Ankara

GALATIA

Dorylaion

Pessinius

CAPPADOCIA

PHRYGIA

Antioch of Pisidia

Iconium
Konya

Lystra

Derbe

Tarsus

TAURUS MOUNTAINS

PISIDIA

LYCAONIA

CILICIA

Antioch

Seleucia
Pieria

PAMPHYLIA

Attalia
Antalya

SYRIA

LYCIA

Patara

Myra
Kale

Salamis

CYPRUS

Byblos

PHOENICIA

Paphos

Sidon

Tyre

Ptolemais
Acre

SAMARIA

MEDITERRANEAN SEA

Caesarea

Jerusalem

JUDEA

Philippi

Paul and his companions were now in Europe. Philippi was on the *Via Egnatia* which passed through an imposing triumphal arch in the city. This great artery connecting the heart of Rome with its eastern members was constructed by Gnaeus Egnatius, one of the early governors of Macedonia, in the second century BC and it stretched from Dyrrachium on the Adriatic coast (whence ships sailed to Italy) to Neapolis on the shores of the Aegean Sea. Later it was extended through Thrace to Byzantium (Istanbul), a total distance of about 696 miles (1,120 km). Philippi was founded in 356 BC by Philip of Macedon, father of Alexander the Great, who used gold and silver from the region to finance his military campaigns, and those of his son. The mines are said to have produced the considerable income of one thousand talents a year.

The town was also the site of a decisive battle in the Roman Civil War in 42 BC when Mark Antony and Octavian defeated Brutus and Cassius, the last of the Republicans, and assassins of Julius Caesar. In Shakespeare's drama Caesar's ghost appears to Brutus with a sinister warning of defeat: *"Thou shalt see me at Philippi."* In due course history credited Octavian as the victor and this was duly celebrated by an imposing triumphal arch through which passed the *Via Egnatia*.

Looking southwest towards the Plain of Philippi where a battle in 42 BC led to the end of the Roman Republic. The ruins of the Roman forum are in the centre of the picture.

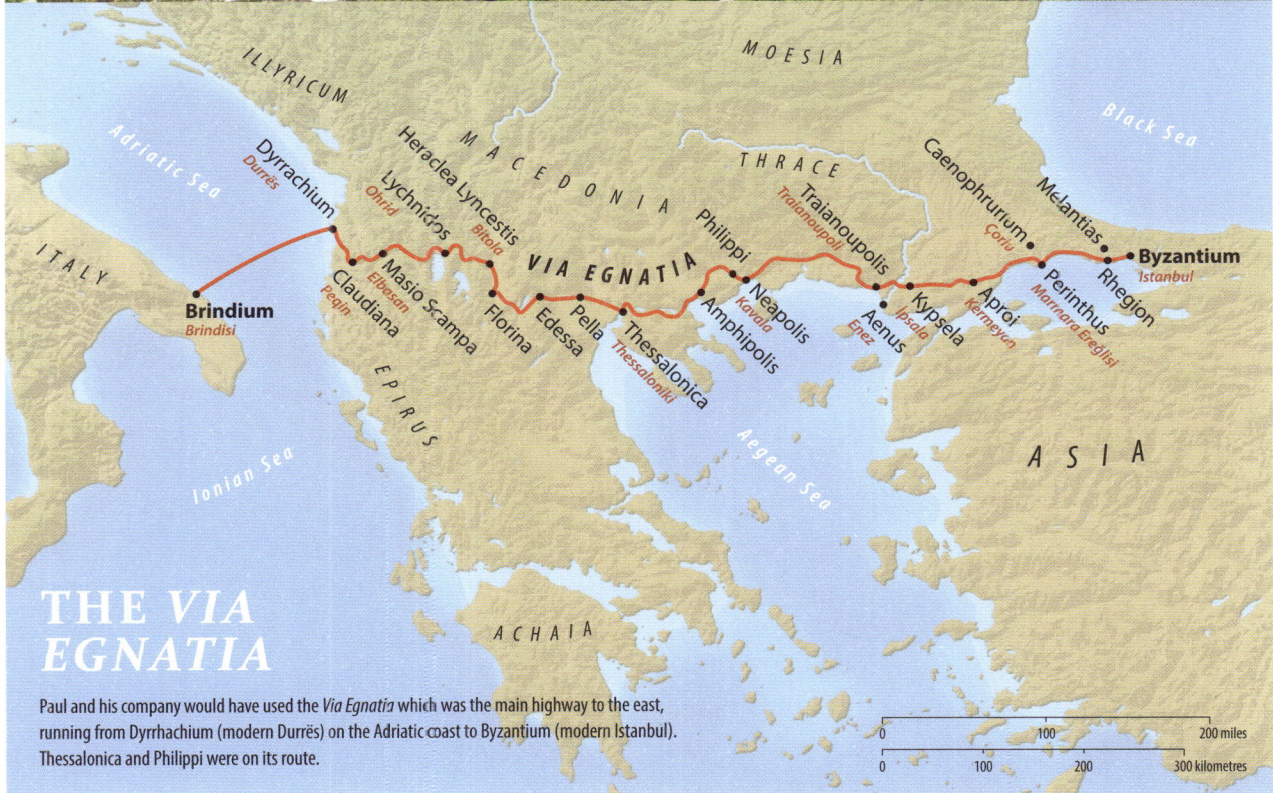

THE *VIA EGNATIA*

Paul and his company would have used the *Via Egnatia* which was the main highway to the east, running from Dyrrhachium (modern Durrës) on the Adriatic coast to Byzantium (modern Istanbul). Thessalonica and Philippi were on its route.

The battle of Philippi had far reaching results for western civilisation. It left the Second Triumvirate, Octavian, Mark Anthony and Marcus Lepidus joint rulers of the Roman world. By 27 BC Octavian had risen to supremacy, was given the title *Gaius Julius Caesar Augustus* by the Senate and began to rule over what became known as the Roman Empire. In Biblical prophecy this empire was the *fourth beast, dreadful and terrible* (Daniel 7: 7), and the beast and false prophet (Revelation 19: 20) have been identified as the political descendants of Augustus. It was in his reign that Jesus was born and, a few years later, Paul.

Five years after the battle the victors, Mark Antony and Octavian, settled many veteran soldiers in Philippi and made it a Roman colony so it became politically part of Rome. Local government was in the hands of two annually appointed magistrates called *praetors*, and Philippians were intensely proud of their Roman status. The population at the time of Paul's visit is thought to have been five to ten thousand.

The river where Lydia and her companions gathered for prayer may have been the Gangites (shown here) or a tributary stream, the Krenides.

purple

Lydia must have had considerable capital if she traded in purple (*porphyra*), either the dye or garments. Usually obtained from shellfish such as *murex*, it was a luxury item, much in demand in Rome. The colour was also called crimson. Different purple stripes denoted the status of Senators and Equestrians, and purple was the colour of emperors – hence the purple robe put on Christ, in mockery. Thyatira was famous for its dyeing, and inscriptions indicate there was a guild of purple sellers. The industry there continued into the nineteenth century before being superseded by chemical dyes.

On the Sabbath Paul and his companions visited a site by the river, possibly the River Gangites, where persons gathered for prayer. The Jewish population in Philippi was evidently too small to sustain a synagogue (the quorum being ten Jewish men) so the Jews met where water was available for purification, together with Gentile 'worshippers'. One of these was Lydia, a woman from Thyatira, in Asia Minor, who sold the purple for which her city was famous. She received the knowledge of Christ through Paul's word, becoming the first convert to Christianity in Europe, and offered her house to Paul for accommodation.

Paul in prison

Paul's service at Philippi was hindered by a female slave having the spirit of Python, who followed them around with flattering cries. After enduring this for many days the apostle turned, and enjoined the spirit to leave her in the name of Jesus Christ. The slave became calm, but her owners, who had made money out of her prophetic utterances, resented the sudden termination of their income. They vented their anger against Paul, dragging him and Silas before the magistrates, the character of Satanic opposition changing abruptly from subtle flattery to open hatred. The charges laid before the *praetors* were false, but they aroused the pride of the Roman crowd. Their prejudice against Jews was directed at Paul and Silas so that the *praetors* took the easy way out. Without bothering to hear any defence they tore off the clothes of the accused and ordered them to be scourged. The sentence was duly executed by the *lictors*, officials who attended and guarded Roman magistrates. They carried bundles of rods – *fasces* (the origin of *fascist*) – which sometimes included an axe, symbolising the power to execute. *Lictors* were invariably strongly built men and the punishment of many stripes was evidently severe. As well as the physical suffering there was the degradation of a public beating, which Paul refers to in 1 Thessalonians 2: 2. This was no doubt one of the three times the Apostle was scourged by the Gentiles (2 Corinthians 11: 25).

Roman prisons were terrible places, used primarily to hold people awaiting trial or execution. The inner prison where Paul and Silas were confined was probably below ground level, damp and in darkness. Their feet were locked in stocks, which would allow no change of position to alleviate their pain. Unconquered, Paul and Silas praised God with singing, at midnight, to the astonishment of the listening prisoners who were used, no doubt, to hearing only groans and curses. This may have been a habitual act of worship (Psalm 119: 62). The *great earthquake* (Acts 16: 26) loosened the prisoners' chains, which were probably secured to iron rings in the stonework, and led to the conversion of the jailor and his household. This followed Paul's timely intervention to stop him taking his own life in anticipation of the death sentence that invariably followed when a jailor allowed his prisoners to escape. So the jailor was saved from the point of death, and despair turned to joy as he and his house were baptised. Conversion changed his character: tenderly he washed the congealed blood from the raw weals left by the *fasces*, and laid the table for the men who had saved his life. He was Paul's first European convert: Lydia, although the first convert in Europe, was from Asia, so apparently not a European.

fasces
The fasces carried by the lictors were symbols of government as well as implements for chastisement. Since the Roman Empire ended they have been used as an icon of power by numerous governments, including Mussolini's Fascists. Fasces appear on the reverse side of the US 'Mercury' dime, and a pair of crossed fasces is included on the official seal of the US Senate and on the US National Guard Bureau insignia, pictured above.

Civis Romanus Sum
Paul and Silas need only have cried out *Civis Romanus Sum (I am a Roman citizen)* to have avoided punishment at Philippi. It seems the apostle chose to submit to the pain and degradation of a public beating rather than use this way of escape, but he nevertheless testified later to the Magistrates about the illegality of their action. This would have protected the future testimony in Philippi.

the jailor
It was recognised that a jailor forfeited his own life if he allowed one of his prisoners to escape. If he then pre-empted execution by suicide this was favourably regarded by the government. In recognition that the action had saved the cost of a trial, the widow would be allowed to inherit her husband's estate without penalty.

When the *lictors* arrived the following morning with instructions for the jailor to release the two prisoners, Paul sent them back to their masters pointing out that they had publicly beaten and imprisoned Roman citizens, and condemned them without a trial. The *praetors* were alarmed when they heard this, and well they might be! The *Lex Porcia* exempted Roman citizens from degrading punishments and its breach was a capital offence: in the first century a Roman citizen had an absolute exemption from being beaten or held in chains by a public authority. The praetors had acted illegally and were forced to come personally and make acknowledgement. Paul insisted on this for the protection of the gospel, although he had submitted to the punishment. He and Silas went to Lydia's house before leaving the city and the reference to *the brethren* (Acts 16: 40) shows there were also other converts. Luke evidently stayed in Philippi, the narrative changing back to 'they' instead of 'we'. Apparently he does not join Paul's company again until Acts 20: 6, at Troas, five years later.

The salvation of whole households – Cornelius, Lydia and the jailor – was a feature of Gentile conversions, and included baptism as confirmation of their reception into the Christian faith. The Gentile opposition at Philippi was defeated, and Paul left an assembly there which showed him great affection, twice sending him gifts when he was in Thessalonica (Philippians 4: 16).

MACEDONIA AND ACHAIA

10

Paul's second western journey – part two

Thessalonica and Berea

It says much for Paul's stamina and courage that he could set out from Philippi on a journey of around 100 miles (161 km) so soon after being beaten and imprisoned. With Silas he followed the *Via Egnatia*, passing through Amphipolis and Apollonia, until reaching Thessalonica. This port had a large Jewish population and a synagogue that was probably central for the district.

Thessalonica had been given the status of a free city in 42 BC after backing the winning side in the battle of Philippi. This meant the city was self governing and not subject to interference from the Romans, although the governor of Macedonia resided there. Luke, with characteristic accuracy, notes that the city magistrates were called by the special title of *politarchs*. In 146 BC Macedonia was made a single province, with Thessalonica its capital. The city was well placed: the *Via Egnatia* was crossed by routes north to the Danube, and south into northern Greece, and it had an excellent harbour, making it a busy centre of commerce. It is notable that Paul chose large and important cities to work in. There was nothing apologetic about his approach.

At Thessalonica Paul followed his practice of preaching in the synagogue. On three successive Sabbaths he reasoned from the Scriptures that Jesus was the Christ. Jason, his host, if he was the same person named in Romans 16: 21 may have been related to the apostle. Some Jews believed, and many Gentiles, but the unbelieving Jews enlisted a rabble to incite public opinion, and stormed the house of Jason to seize the apostle and his companions. Frustrated in this they dragged Jason and others before the magistrates, accusing them of disloyalty to Caesar by preaching Jesus as another King, the same specious argument used against Christ to Pilate (John 19: 12). This was a serious allegation in the early years of the empire: to proclaim another king amounted to *Crimen Maiestatis*, crime against the emperor, which was treason, and the Jews were already under suspicion from the Romans at this time after insurrections by nationalists. The magistrates however, wiser than those at Philippi, merely took security from Jason and others but did not confine them, and the brethren immediately sent Paul and Silas away, for their own safety. It is not clear how long they had been at Thessalonica, but the Philippians apparently ministered to Paul twice during his service there (Philippians 4: 16).

Leaving Timothy behind, Paul and Silas left at night to start a journey of 48 miles (77 km) to Berea which Cicero referred to as an *oppidium devium*, an out-of-the-way town. It lay south of the *Via Egnatia*, at the foot of Mount Bermius. Undeterred by events at Thessalonica, Paul preached in the synagogue and found the Jews more receptive. Many believed, subjecting their minds to the word, and searching the Scriptures for confirmation. Greeks also were converted, but after Jews from Thessalonica arrived and started to stir up the crowds Paul had to leave. He was escorted to the coast and he and some companions boarded a ship for Athens. Probably they sailed from Dium, 45 miles (72 km) from Berea, past the snow capped Mount Olympus, 9,573 feet (2,918 metres) the "abode of gods" celebrated in Greek mythology. Then, following the coastline of Eastern Greece they would have sailed past the island of Euboea, around the Cape of Sunium and into the Saronic Gulf to the Piraeus – a voyage of around 300 miles (483 km).

Thessalonica

Thessalonica was named after the wife of Cassander, ruler of Macedon, who was half sister of Alexander the Great.

Looking south from Thessalonica to snow capped Mount Olympus, the highest mountain in Greece. In Greek mythology the mountain was regarded as the home of the twelve Olympians, the principal gods of the Classical Greek and Hellenistic worlds.

It would be hard to map a route with more magnificent natural beauty, but there is no indication it affected the apostle, every nerve of whose being was concentrated in the service of his Master. Paul's companions then returned leaving him alone in Athens to wait for Silas and Timothy.

It is noticeable the Jewish opposition was concentrated against Paul personally, forcing him to move on from one city to another. Far from restricting the apostle this simply had the effect of spreading the testimony.

It looks as if a violent persecution broke out against the Thessalonian believers soon after Paul left (1 Thessalonians 2: 14). The apostle, anxious to know if this had undermined the faith of his new converts, made two attempts to return (1 Thessalonians 2: 18). Possibly the security imposed on Jason by the politarchs prevented this. Paul was so concerned that as soon as Silas and Timothy arrived at Athens he sent Timothy back to Thessalonica to find out how things stood (1 Thessalonians 3: 2) and when he returned to Athens with a positive report (1 Thessalonians 3: 6) Paul wrote his first letter to the Thessalonians. This is the first letter from Paul of which we have a record. It is of particular interest in that it was written only a short time after the Thessalonians had been converted to Christianity. By contrast, Paul's letters that have been preserved to us written to other assemblies were composed a considerable time after those assemblies had become established.

Athens was over 300 miles (483 km) away from Thessalonica by road and would have taken Timothy more than two weeks if he went on foot, but less if he used transport or went by sea. Silas and Timothy seem to have been on a further visit to Macedonia, of which we have no record, before joining Paul at Corinth (Acts 18: 5).

Athens – city of culture

Paul was left alone in Athens after Timothy had returned to Thessalonica (1 Thessalonians 3: 1). It is not clear where Silas went. Five centuries previously Athens had been the most celebrated city in the ancient world, renowned for its art, drama, statesmen and schools of philosophy. It had, however, declined since the Roman occupation in 146 BC. The Roman general, Sulla, devastated the city in 88 BC, and Augustus organised the peninsula as the Province of Achaia in 27 BC. However Athens remained a free city and centre of learning and philosophy, patronised by leaders of

Roman society, although rivalled by the schools at Alexandria and Tarsus. Its citizens lived in idleness, proud of the faded glory of their city's golden age and interested in any novelties which would relieve the monotony of their existence.

The Parthenon Temple on the Acropolis of Athens was completed in 438 BC and dedicated to the mythical Greek goddess Athena. It is only a short distance from Mars Hill where Paul told the Areopagites that *The God who has made the world and all things which are in it...does not dwell in temples made with hands* (Acts 17: 24) and offered them a way of escape from idolatry through repentance.

The apostle was grieved by the extent of idolatry in Athens. It was manifest in every direction he looked. The Acropolis, a steep hill dominating the city, was crowned by the Parthenon temple, its bronze colossus of the goddess Athena visible from far out to sea. A forest of statues covered the sides and summit of the Acropolis as well as the streets and public areas – Pliny estimated there were twenty thousand of them – commemorating great men and deified heroes. And on all hands were innumerable shrines and altars dedicated to a vast selection of pagan deities. The apostle first visited the synagogue and reasoned with the Jews, and with Gentile worshippers, and also with those he met in the market place, the Agora, centre of civic life. Philosophers attacked him. Others called him a chatterer. And some apparently misconstrued his preaching, concluding that Jesus and the Resurrection were two new gods. The result was that Paul was taken to the Areopagus – apparently with some degree of duress, since they laid hold of him – and invited to explain his doctrine. Areopagus was once the supreme court of Athens, which sat on Mars Hill, a rocky outcrop of the Acropolis. It guarded the morals, education and religion of the Athenians. Here Socrates came to face his accusers in 399 BC. At the time of Paul's visit its authority was diminished so that it was little more than a forum for political debate. The apostle appeared as an apologist – defending a position by argument – rather than as an accused person.

Greek writers
In his apology to the Areopagus Paul quotes the Cretan philosopher Epimenedes 'for in him we live and move and exist', who is also the author of the quotation in Titus 1: 12. The author of the quotation 'we are also his offspring' is Aratus the Cilician.

Paul's address to the Areopagites

Paul's address, which Luke summarises, shows inspired skill in gaining and holding the interest of his hearers. The teaching, had they heeded it, would have recovered them to the knowledge of the true God, which they had lost in the delusion of idolatry.

The altar which Paul observed is said to have originated when a fatal epidemic raged in the city. The inhabitants, having in vain consulted their gods for relief, were advised by an oracle to dedicate an altar to the unknown God. Paul skilfully built on the link to introduce the one true God, the Originator of life and providential governor of the universe, truths that conflicted with the evolutionary theories of the Epicureans. He strengthened his link with his audience by quoting poets that would be familiar to them, Epimenides of Crete, and the Cilician, Aratus, and then used the references to expose the nature of idolatry and manifest the true God to their consciences. The accusers of Paul were thus convicted themselves, but repentance was an alien idea to these proud, intellectual Athenians and some openly mocked at the reference to resurrection. A few, however, were prepared to take the way of escape offered in repentance. Dionysius was no doubt an older man. One qualification for an Areopagite was to be over the age of sixty.

EPICUREANS AND STOICS

Paul's audience would have included followers of the Epicurean and Stoic philosophies. The former subscribed to the teachings of Epicurus, 341–270 BC, who made no allowance for creation and taught that matter had evolved into its present forms; that death ended existence; that the gods were remote from man and uncaring; and that attainment of pleasure and avoidance of pain were the most worthy human pursuits. The Stoics, founded by Zeno, 335–263 BC, taught pantheism – that God exists in everything; acknowledged what was divine as the animating principle of the universe; had a rigid scheme of morals; and believed that true wisdom lay in accepting and adjusting to the inevitable, and indifference to pleasure or pain.

The Areopagus, where Paul addressed the Athenians, is a bare outcrop of marble known as Mars Hill, and the name also designates the assembly which sat there, which was at one time the council of the city elders, and a court of appeal. Although there was scant response to Paul's speech at the time, his words are today engraved in bronze at the base of Areopagus, symbolic of the enduring victory of Christianity over paganism.

So Paul left Athens with little outward result: the proud culture of the city proved barren ground for the seed of his glad tidings, whereas in the commercial centre of Corinth, with all its moral disorder, a large assembly would flourish.

Corinth – city of commerce

Paul, evidently still alone, travelled from Athens to Corinth, probably by sea across the Saronic Gulf which would have taken less than a day, then eight miles (13 km) by road from Cenchrea. The alternative route overland was about fifty miles (80 km). After Eleusis it followed the so-called *Sacred Way* into the city.

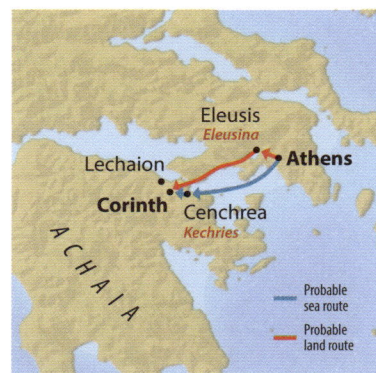

two harbours
Strabo, the Greek geographer, in his work *Geography* noted the commercial advantage of the city, *"Corinth is called 'wealthy' because of its commerce, since it is situated on the Isthmus and is master of two harbours, of which the one leads straight to Asia, and the other to Italy; and it makes easy the exchange of merchandise from both countries that are so far distant from each other."*

The city he arrived at was built on a plain, but dominated by the Acrocorinth, a monolithic rock which rose steeply to 1,885 feet (575 metres). It was strategically situated on the isthmus linking mainland Greece with the Peloponnisos peninsula. This endowed it with two harbours. Lechaion, on the west, gave access to the central and western Mediterranean, through the Gulf of Corinth, whilst Cenchrea, on the east, was a base for the Aegean Sea, Black Sea and eastern Mediterranean. It was natural to think of a canal across the isthmus to avoid shipping having to sail around the dangerous peninsula. Several attempted such a project, but it was not to be completed until 1893. In Paul's time, however, smaller ships were portaged three and a half miles (6 km) between the two harbours on a roadway made of logs, the *dialkos*.

Cenchrea was Corinth's eastern harbour. Phoebe served in the assembly here, and was commended by Paul (Romans 16: 1).

Apart from its harbours, Corinth commanded the north/south land route, and was blessed with an abundant water supply, so it is not surprising it had become the third largest port in the Graeco-Roman world. The city was also noted for its architecture and the *Corinthian* order of architecture which was developed in the Classical Greek Era became the third order, after the *Ionic* and *Doric*. Its ornate style was in ironic contrast to the simplicity of the apostle's tents.

The renowned Doric columns in the sixth century BC Temple of Apollo at Corinth must have contrasted with the simplicity of the tents made by Paul. The temple overlooked the agora (marketplace) and originally had thirty-eight columns.

The Roman General Lucius Mummius devastated Corinth in 146 BC to punish the city for having rebelled against Rome. He massacred her citizens, razed the fine buildings and made off with the art treasures. In 46 BC, shortly before he was assassinated, Julius Caesar started to rebuild Corinth, gave it the status of a colony, and populated it with veterans and freedmen. The city became the capital of Achaia and seat of Roman administration for the Province.

The Lechaion Way linked Corinth's western port, Lechaion, to the city. Phoebe would probably have sailed from Lechaion to travel to Rome.

In Paul's time Corinth was a bustling and successful centre of commerce, indeed the trading centre of Greece. The city was much larger than Athens with a cosmopolitan population. Corinth hosted the Isthmian Games every two years, in which all Greek cities took part. Paul's imagery in his epistles included references which the Corinthians would understand such as running and boxing (1 Corinthians 9: 24–27). The city was also known for its profligacy so that the very name Corinthian became a synonym for licentiousness. This was due partly to a high influx of sailors and slaves, and also because of the worship of *Aphrodite*, goddess of love. Her temple, with its ritual immorality, was on the summit of Acrocorinth. This was no doubt a legacy from the Phoenicians, original founders of Corinth, and their worship of *Astarte* (*Ashtoreth* in the Old Testament – see 2 Kings 23: 13, also Genesis 38: 21 note *b* in J. N. Darby Bible). It was from this unlikely background that Paul's converts were drawn. But it proved more fruitful than the proud scepticism of Athens.

Paul's resolve to meet his own expenses while at Corinth brought him into contact with Aquila and Priscilla. They had left Italy after Emperor Claudius banned all Jews from Rome around 50 AD. Three of the six Scriptural

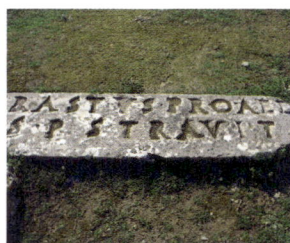

This inscription has been translated as: *Erastus in return for his aedileship laid (the pavement) at his own expense*. The *aedile* was the city magistrate in charge of public works and roads. It may be this was the same Erastus referred to in Romans 16: 23 (see also Acts 19: 22, 2 Timothy 4: 20).

PAUL'S FINANCES

Travel in Paul's day involved expense. There were regular tolls on the roads, especially at bridges, apart from the cost of overnight accommodation, and the hire of beasts or transport. Then of course there was the cost of food and subsistence. Sea travel was also expensive.

Although Paul evidently accepted Lydia's hospitality at Philippi, at Thessalonica and elsewhere he insisted on paying his way, refusing to depend on charity even although he had the right, as an apostle, to do so. He chose not to exercise this right (1 Corinthians 9: 12, 18) in order to make the glad tidings costless to others. This meant he sometimes had to do secular work at night, as well as during the day (1 Thessalonians 2: 9, 2 Thessalonians 3: 8) in addition to his evangelical ministry. It is extraordinary to think of the apostle to the nations having to undertake physical labour so that he could meet his expenses without being dependent on his brethren.

The apostle's secular work was evidently tent making, or leather working, which could be set up easily in any location. There is no doubt Paul would have been an expert craftsman, and would have known where there was a market for what he could produce.

The brethren at Philippi sent two contributions to Paul at Thessalonica (Philippians 4: 16). Paul also worked at tent making at Corinth (Acts 18: 3) but his ministry there was partly financed by gifts from assemblies or individuals in Macedonia (2 Corinthians 11: 8,9). He came under criticism from rivals who claimed that the fact that he worked indicated he was not an apostle, which he answers in 1 Corinthians 9. One of his reasons for not accepting gifts from the wealthy Corinthians was to counter the false teachers. Paul also worked while at Ephesus – see 1 Corinthians 4: 11, 12; and Acts 20: 34.

Paul tells the Philippians that he had suffered the loss of all (3: 8). At the time of his arrest, however, he did not appear to be under financial pressure. He financed the four men who made a vow, in Jerusalem, and later Festus hoped to receive bribes from him, evidently suspecting he had means. When in Rome there were the expenses of his hired lodging and the costs of his legal defence, which might have been considerable where an appeal to the emperor was involved. It may be these expenses were met by ministrations from the assemblies.

references to the couple put Priscilla's name first. Some have speculated she may have been a Gentile, connected with the *gens prisca*, one of the leading families in Rome. They were tentmakers, and Paul lived and worked with them. It is evident that Aquila and Priscilla were already believers, but we do not know how or when the assembly in Rome started.

After the Jews refused Paul's teaching in the synagogue he left them, and lodged with a Gentile worshipper, Justus. However Crispus, the Jewish ruler of the synagogue, believed, followed by many Corinthians, and Paul had a vision from the Lord strengthening him in his work, after which he taught for a further eighteen months.

Looking north across the Gulf of Corinth from the Acrocorinth, a rocky outcrop rising above the city.

Christianity at Rome
According to the Roman historian Seutonius, Claudius expelled the Jews from Rome on account of their continual tumults, instigated by Chrestus (Claudius, c. 25). This suggests that Christianity had by then become established in the capital, possibly taken there by the Romans, both Jews and proselytes, who were in Jerusalem at Pentecost (Acts 2: 10). The greetings in Romans 16 show that Paul knew many of the brethren in Rome before he visited the city.

Gallio's judgement

A change of proconsul in the Province gave the malevolent Jews the opportunity they sought against Paul. They dragged him before the judgement seat with an accusation of teaching an illegal religion. Judaism was a *religio licita*, a permitted religion, and their case was that Paul's teaching departed from it, so was illegal. The new proconsul, Annaeus Gallio, was brother of Lucius Seneca, the Stoic philosopher who was one of Nero's counsellors during his early reign, and was known as *dulcis Gallio* because of his kindness and generosity. However he saw through the animosity of the Jews, whom he despised, and did not even trouble to listen to Paul's defence, thus missing the opportunity of a lifetime of hearing the apostle speak. He rightly judged, however, that the issue was not one that affected Roman law, and it was not part of his office to judge Jewish questions. He unceremoniously cleared the accusers from the judgement-seat, at which the bystanders turned on Sosthenes, the ruler of the synagogue, and beat him publicly. Gallio callously ignored this lawless action. This was the first case testing the legal status of the Christian faith in the first century. Gallio's ruling confirmed that Christianity continued to shelter under the same legal protection as Judaism, and established an important precedent. Had it been otherwise Paul's service could have been restricted. In later years Christians were persecuted under the law *Religio nova et illicita* – a new and illegal religion.

After some time Paul sailed from Cenchrea to Ephesus, a voyage of about 220 miles (354 km) which would have taken two or three days. Aquila and Priscilla went with him as far as Ephesus, and relocated there, returning to Rome after the death of the Emperor Claudius. Paul reasoned with the Jews at Ephesus but refused their invitation to stay on. He insisted he wanted to keep the coming feast at Jerusalem, but promised to return. The feast was probably the Passover, and Paul had taken a vow. The opposition of the Jews did not diminish his respect for his nation, and its place before God. From Ephesus the route followed the coast of Asia Minor, past the islands of Cos and Rhodes, then across the open sea, past Cyprus, to Caesarea, a voyage of about 650 miles (1,046 km). Caesarea to Jerusalem was a further 62 miles (100 km) Luke's only comment on the apostle's fourth visit there since his conversion is that he *saluted the assembly*, and Jerusalem is not actually mentioned in his text. The return journey to Antioch was a further 360 miles (579 km).

Sosthenes

Who was it that beat Sosthenes before the judgement seat? It may have been Gentile bystanders, taking advantage of the discomfiture of the Jews when their case was rejected by Gallio. Alternatively it may have been the Jews themselves. If Sosthenes in Acts 18 is the same person as in 1 Corinthians 1: 1 he may have already manifested Christian sympathies so that the Jews vented their frustration on him. Various manuscripts of Acts 18: 17 have been emended to support one of these viewpoints, but the true reading says *all laid hold on Sosthenes*, as if it was a general uprising. Sosthenes may have been joint ruler of the synagogue with Crispus (Acts 18: 8) or he may have succeeded him.

Philippi back to Antioch in Syria

about 1,850 miles (2,977 km)

Total journey

at least 3,000 miles (4,828 km)

THE PROVINCE OF ASIA

11

Paul's third western journey – part one

The focus of Paul's third missionary journey was to establish assemblies in Ephesus, and in the Province of Asia. Christianity had been inaugurated in Jerusalem. Antioch had been the base for the evangelisation of the Gentiles. Now Asia Minor was to become a centre of operations. Its assemblies were later used by John (Revelation 2, 3) to symbolise the Christian testimony.

A secondary aim was to co-ordinate collections for Judaea. But the apostle's fifth and final visit to Jerusalem led to his arrest, and the end of his public ministry, so far as Luke's account is concerned.

The road to Ephesus

Luke does not tell us who accompanied Paul from Antioch to Ephesus. The last mention of Silvanus by Luke is in Acts 18: 5 when he came to Corinth (see Appendix A: *Paul's Companions*).

To reach Galatia and Phrygia Paul would have taken the route through the Cilician Gates (see page 16), evidently visiting established assemblies. From 1 Corinthians 16: 1 we learn that he gave instructions to the Galatians about the collection. The most direct approach to Ephesus from the north, or north east, was along the valley of the Meander. However this would have taken in Colossae, Laodicea and Hierapolis, whereas Colossians 1: 4 and 2: 1 seem to indicate that Paul had never met the Christians in those places. It is more likely, therefore, that he approached Ephesus from further to the north. Luke compresses the journey from Antioch in Syria to Ephesus, which was over 1,000 miles (1,609 km), into a couple of verses, Acts 18: 23 and Acts 19: 1.

... Paul, having passed through the upper districts, came to Ephesus...
Acts 18: 1

It is thought the population of Ephesus at that time was around 250,000 of which some 10,000 were Jewish, making it the fourth largest city of the empire, after Rome, Alexandria and Antioch in Syria. Although three miles (5 km) from the sea, its excellent harbour, long since silted up, made it one of the world's major ports, used for exports to Rome. Ephesus was the terminus of the great trade route from the east, and was on the main road north to Smyrna, Pergamos and Troas. Famous and wealthy, it was also the residence for the Proconsul, the Governor of Asia, although the official capital of the Province was Pergamos. Culturally the city was a mixture of Greek art and Asiatic mysticism, dominated by the temple of Artemis. Constructed in 550 BC this was the largest building in the Greek world, and one of the seven wonders of the ancient world. It was made entirely from marble, with one hundred and twenty-seven Ionic columns up to fifty-seven feet (17.4 metres) high.

The road to the port at Ephesus, where Paul may have embarked. Ephesus declined after a series of earthquakes, combined with overgrazing and deforestation. Its strategic harbour silted up and the remains of the city are now several miles from the coast.

The Jews in Ephesus had shown interest in Paul's teaching on his first visit (Acts 18: 20). Since then Apollos, from Alexandria, a Jew who had been converted to Christianity, had spoken boldly in the synagogue. Luke describes him as eloquent, mighty in the scriptures and fervent in his spirit. His knowledge, however, was limited to the baptism of John, which implied the need of repentance in order to receive Christ. Aquila and Priscilla, who had remained in the city after accompanying Paul on his first visit, were able to instruct him more exactly. No doubt they conveyed the significance of the death and resurrection of Jesus. Apollos subsequently visited Achaia, with a letter from the brethren at Ephesus commending him. His forceful preaching convinced the Jews, and he showed from the Scriptures that Jesus was the Christ.

No doubt Apollos was used to prepare the ground for Paul. The twelve disciples who had not heard the Holy Spirit had come were presumably converts of Apollos, and after baptising them the apostle spoke boldly in the synagogue over three months. When the familiar opposition began he separated the disciples and reasoned daily in the school of Tyrannus, who was probably a teacher of philosophy or rhetoric. According to the Bezae manuscript of the New Testament the apostle used the schoolroom in the heat of the day, equivalent to the hours between 11 and 4. This is credible, since Greeks and Romans started their day at dawn, and late morning to early evening was a time of siesta. During these two years of reasoning the word was heard throughout Asia. From Revelation 2 and 3 we know of six other assemblies in the Province, all of which were commercial centres. According to Romans 16: 5, Epaenetus was one of the first converts in Asia.

The power of the ministry at Ephesus is evident in Luke's account. God wrought no ordinary miracles by the hands of Paul. The seven sons of Sceva were exposed, believers came confessing and declaring their deeds, and practitioners of curious arts burnt their books. However these results involved suffering on the part of the apostle. Paul's image of a gladiator fighting wild beasts in the arena (1 Corinthians 15: 32) gives a hint of the opposition he experienced, which is confirmed by 1 Corinthians 16: 9 – the adversaries many. And 2 Corinthians 1 and 4 indicate the persecution may have been much more violent, and continued longer than is recorded by Luke. This reminds us that

PAUL'S THIRD WESTERN JOURNEY – PART ONE

Ephesus

Smyrna

Pergamos

Thyatira

Sardis

Philadelphia

Laodicea

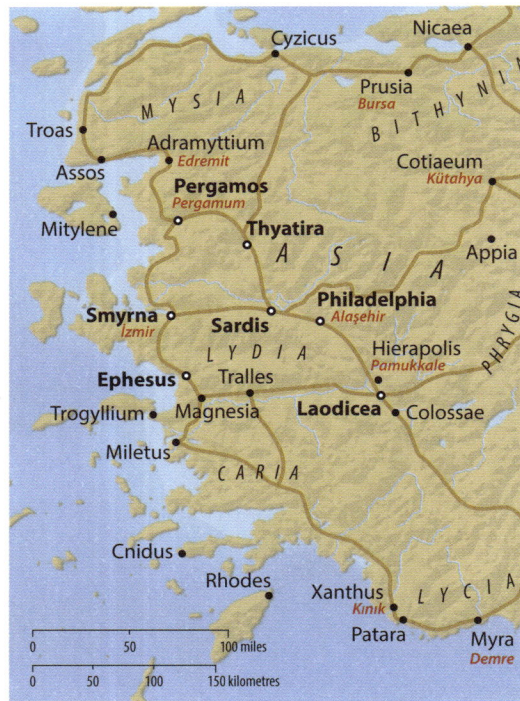

Acts is a skilful selection of events, and not everything is included. For example Romans 16: 7 refers to Andronicus and Junias as Paul's fellow captives. Since Romans was written from Corinth, following Paul's time at Ephesus, this could refer to some imprisonment during this period, of which we have no record. The reference in Romans 16: 3 to *Prisca and Aquila... who for my life staked their own neck* may also refer to some risk they took during this time to save Paul, perhaps in giving him protection during the riot at Ephesus.

This riot was instigated by Demetrius, a silver-beater, whose inflammatory words incited the artisans and the entire city. It was a further attack against the apostle (Acts 19: 26). The theatre of Ephesus, where the crowds thronged, was capable of holding twenty-four thousand people on its steeply raked seating and the collective fury of such a large assembly must have been terrifying. Paul, never lacking courage, would have gone in to the crowd for the sake of Gaius and Aristarchus, who had been seized, had he not been restrained by the disciples and by some of the Asiarchs who were his friends. Asiarchs were presidents of the games and festivals, selected annually from the wealthiest citizens of the chief cities of the province. Probably they were in Ephesus for a festival connected with the goddess Artemis. The mob refused to listen to Alexander, spokesman for the Jews, a sad proof that this ancient people had lost all their moral power through opposing the gospel. After heeding the calming words of the town clerk the crowds eventually dispersed. The opposition had burned itself out and achieved nothing.

Paul's long service at Ephesus did not change his care for all the assemblies. He wrote the first letter to the Corinthians from Ephesus and sent it at the hands of Titus (2 Corinthians 12: 18). He also sent Timothy to serve in Macedonia, and tells the Corinthians how to receive him if he went on to Corinth (1 Corinthians 16: 10).

The Roman theatre at Ephesus, scene of the
tumult described in Acts 19, could accommodate
some twenty-four thousand people.

A meeting with Titus

Adverse reports of conditions at Corinth must have added to Paul's burdens while he was at Ephesus. His original intention was to go directly from Ephesus to Corinth by ship. He would then proceed to Macedonia, and return again to Corinth before leaving for Judaea (Acts 19: 21, 2 Corinthians 1: 15). Instead he wrote the first epistle to the Corinthians and sent it at the hand of Titus, and arranged to go to Macedonia first. His change of plan was evidently criticised by some at Corinth (2 Corinthians 1: 17). Some authorities think that 1 Corinthians 5: 9 indicates there was a further letter to the Corinthians which has not been preserved to us.

The great apostle was evidently under relentless pressure at this time. In his second letter to the Corinthians he refers to:

> ...our tribulation which happened to us in Asia, that we were excessively pressed beyond our power, so as to despair even of living. (2 Corinthians 1: 8)

We do not know whether this refers to the riot at Ephesus, or other traumatic events. In addition Paul was deeply anxious as to how his first letter to the Corinthians had been received. The early chapters of Paul's second letter to the Corinthians bring out the intensity of exercise which was so characteristic of him.

But he who encouragers those that are brought low, even God, encouraged us by the coming of Titus...

2 Corinthians 7: 6

After instructing Timothy, who remained at Ephesus (1 Timothy 1: 3), the apostle left for Troas. He probably travelled by sea, a journey of about 175 miles (282 km) and waited there for Titus. Although he found a positive response to his preaching at Troas his anxiety for the Corinthians led him to move on to Macedonia (2 Corinthians 2: 12, 13). No doubt he went by ship to Neapolis, a voyage of 138 miles (222 km). Eventually he met Titus somewhere in Macedonia, and his report from Corinth brought encouragement (2 Corinthians 7: 5–7). Paul's intense relief is evident: in the first chapter of his second letter to the Corinthians he makes nine references to encouragement. Titus was then sent back to Corinth with this letter, with two other brothers who are unnamed, but referred to in 2 Corinthians 8: 18 and 22. The brother whose praise is in the glad tidings may have been Luke. Titus himself is mentioned nine times in this epistle.

Illyricum and the Adriatic coast

The Roman province of Illyricum bordered with the northwest frontier of Macedonia, and then extended down the Adriatic coast. In Romans 15: 19 Paul declares that *I, from Jerusalem, and in a circuit round to Illyricum, have fully preached the glad tidings of the Christ*. He uses the Latin form of Illyricum in writing to Romans, rather than the Greek *Illyria*. Although the preposition *to* may mean *as far as* it seems probable that Paul went into Illyricum and the journey is most likely to have taken place between his visits to Macedonia and Greece (Acts 20: 2). This verse is compressed, but it is thought the period between Paul leaving Ephesus and arriving in Greece may be around eighteen months. The most direct route to Illyricum from Macedonia would be along the *Via Egnatia* westwards from Philippi to Dyrrhachium (modern Dürres, Albania) on the Adriatic coast, a journey of 326 miles (525 km). But Paul might also have travelled north, into modern Bulgaria, perhaps as far as the Danube, before turning west. And he may well have gone further up the Adriatic coast. A later reference to Dalmatia (2 Timothy 4: 10), which was to the north west of Illyricum, indicates there was a testimony in those parts.

Syrian Antioch to Ephesus & Corinth, including Illyricum

2,300 miles (3,701 km)

The Roman province of Illyricum bordered on the Adriatic, and Paul would most likely have reached it by the *Via Egnatia* which terminated at the coastal city of Dyrrhachium (modern Dürres, Albania). This picture is of Budva, north of Dürres, in modern Montenegro.

Winter in Greece

The three months spent in Greece were probably during the winter
(1 Corinthians 16: 6) before the seas opened for a return voyage to Judea.
From Romans 16: 23 we learn that Paul stayed with Gaius at Corinth.
But we have no information how he was received by the Corinthians,
after his two letters to them. During this time Paul wrote the Epistle to the
Romans, which may have been taken to Rome by Phoebe (Romans 16: 1, 2).
In chapter 15: 24 Paul tells the Romans of his plans to visit them on his
way to Spain, once he had delivered the collection to Jerusalem. However
the apostle's foreboding is apparent when he asks them to pray that he
may be saved from those that do not believe in Judea (Romans 15: 31).

In his second letter to Corinth Paul makes two references to a third visit.
However this letter was written from Macedonia before the three month
visit above, so the three month visit is the second visit to Corinth recorded
by Luke, the first being his original visit on his second western journey
(Acts 18: 1). This has led some to wonder if there was a previous visit to
Corinth, not recorded by Luke.

The collection for Jerusalem

Paul organised collections for the Jerusalem saints in fulfilment of
his commitment to James, Cephas and John to remember the poor
(Galatians 2: 10). The original practice of having all things common
(Acts 2: 44) does not appear to have made the assembly at Jerusalem self
sufficient. James 2: 5 suggests there were a number of poor brethren there.
Some saints had been put in prison during the persecution following
the death of Stephen, and Judea suffered in the severe famine during
the reign of Claudius. Relief of poverty was not Paul's only motive. He
also saw the collection as helping to heal any differences between Jewish
and Gentile Christians. Although the collection is only once mentioned
in Acts (24: 17) Paul's enthusiasm in co-ordinating it is seen from his
epistles. To stimulate giving he uses the Galatians as an example to the
Corinthians (1 Corinthians 16: 1), he uses the Corinthians as an example to
the Macedonians (2 Corinthians 9: 2); and he uses both the Corinthians
and Macedonians as examples to the Romans (Romans 15: 26). The
total sum collected must have been considerable and the danger in
transportation very great. No doubt the money collected would be
exchanged for gold to reduce the volume although it is also possible it
may have been in the form of a draft.

"BOUND IN MY SPIRIT I GO TO JERUSALEM"

12

Paul's third western journey – part two

After spending three winter months in Greece, Paul was ready to return to Jerusalem. From Romans 15: 28 it seems that the apostle regarded his forthcoming visit there with the collections as a conclusion to his ministry in Asia and elsewhere. He then intended to start a new mission to Rome and Spain. March 5th was the start of the sailing season in much of the Mediterranean, following the festival of *Navigium Isidis*, and the original intention was to sail from Cenchrea to Syria, probably on a ship taking Jews from the provinces to celebrate the Passover. This had to be changed, however, after discovery of a treacherous plot by the Jews against Paul and it was agreed to return through Macedonia. Seven of Paul's companions went on ahead, to Troas. It is probable they had responsibility for the collections from the various assemblies named (Acts 20: 4). The provinces of Galatia, Asia and Macedonia are represented, but not Achaia, possibly because Paul was carrying the Corinthians' collection himself. Luke evidently joined Paul at Philippi (Acts 20: 5) and they sailed from Neapolis to Troas after the days of unleavened bread. This time the voyage took five days. The wind was evidently not in their favour, as it had been during Paul's second journey (Acts 16: 11).

The number of days between Paul reaching Philippi, and his arrival at Caesarea, has been calculated at around thirty-seven. There are forty-nine days between Passover and Pentecost, and the days of unleavened bread follow the Passover. So there was still a good margin to get from Caesarea to Jerusalem in time for the feast of Pentecost (Acts 20: 16).

Troas

This was Paul's third recorded visit to Troas. He had broken off his preaching on the previous occasion in order to meet Titus (2 Corinthians 2: 12, 13). The mention of the upper room (Acts 20: 8) suggests the congregation was relatively small, and the description of *many lights* shows that the proceedings were not held in secret or in the dark. Although the early Christians broke bread every day (Acts 2: 46) the practice at Troas, and no doubt more generally, was to assemble to break bread on the first day of the week, the day of Christ's resurrection. The weather was hot, the hour was late, many lamps were burning and Paul's discourse was at length. The youth Eutychus, sitting in the window opening, became overpowered by deep sleep and fell from the third storey. Paul, with extraordinary capacity to meet any situation, was first on the scene. Although stunned, the life (soul) of Eutychus had not left his body and through the service of the apostle *they brought away the boy alive*, Acts 20: 12. After breaking the bread, and conversing until daybreak, the disciples boarded a ship for Assos.

Be not troubled, for his life is in him.
Acts 20: 10

PAUL'S WALK FROM TROAS TO ASSOS

The time at Troas included a long discourse, the resuscitation of Eutychus, the celebration of the Lord's Supper and prolonged conversation until daybreak. It seems extraordinary that after this night of activity the apostle should choose to walk by himself to Assos, directing his companions to go by ship. It has been suggested he wanted to be alone as he contemplated what might be the outcome of his visit to Jerusalem. He would probably have followed the coastal road through the villages of Kolonai and Larisa, or he might have taken a more direct route across the high ground, which was not much over 1,000 feet (305 metres). Either way, he would have been able to keep the ship in view most of the time.

The harbour at Assos, where Paul rejoined his companions (Acts 20:14). They had sailed from Troas, while he walked.

Excavations on the site of Troas, where Paul revived Eutychus (Acts 20: 10).

Paul, however, elected to walk from Troas to Assos, where he joined the ship, a distance of about 30 miles (48 km). His preference to be alone at this time, and his extended speaking at Troas, were no doubt because the apostle was preoccupied with the apparent end of his career. His request for the brethren at Rome to pray for him (Romans 15: 30) shows the danger he anticipated at Jerusalem.

A last meeting with the elders of Ephesus

The detail of this voyage, which Luke records as an eyewitness, contrasts with some of his concise summaries when he was not present. His interest in maritime matters is apparent, and his knowledge of ships and travel.

The voyage from Troas to Patara was in a small coasting vessel which sailed from one port to another along the coast. The prevailing wind was from the northwest at this time of the year which was ideal for sailing southwards. However it invariably failed late in the afternoon so they moored for each night and made an early start the following morning. From Assos there was a short run of 32 miles (51 km) to Mitylene, chief city of the island of Lesbos. The next day the travellers were *opposite Chios*, which seems as if they may have been becalmed on the eastern side of this fertile island. They then *put in at Samos* which refers to the port on the southeast of the island. The anchorage, at Trogyllium, was across the narrow strait, just off the mainland.

Mitylene, Lesbos, where Paul's ship called after he had been taken on board (Acts 20: 14).

The next day's voyage to Miletus would have taken only a few hours. The messenger Paul then sent to Ephesus would have sailed across the gulf that then existed, since silted up, to Priene, then across the hills and along the coast to Ephesus. The distance in each direction was about 40 miles (64 km). Paul's discourse to the Ephesian elders, the only record we have of an address by him to Christians, is of immense significance as marking the end of the period of apostolic labours and the start of a new phase with the elders charged to shepherd the assembly of God and maintain what had been established. It is important to notice that Paul does not set on apostolic succession nor an ecclesiastical system. Luke records the ardent affection of the Ephesians for Paul, and their grief that they would not see his face again. His description clearly has the authenticity of an eyewitness.

PAUL'S THIRD WESTERN JOURNEY – PART TWO

Paul goes to Jerusalem – his fifth and final visit

Finally getting away they sailed southwards, with views of the island of Patmos to the east, where John was later exiled by the emperor (probably Nero or Domitian), to anchor for the night at Cos. The island may have had some interest for Luke, the beloved physician, as the traditional birthplace of Hippocrates, (c460 BC–377 BC), and site of the Koan medical school. The next day the travellers reached Rhodes, its celebrated colossus long since toppled and shattered by an earthquake. Looking east to the Lycian mainland they would have seen a majestic cluster of snow capped peaks, the western ranges of the Taurus Mountains. The following day brought them to Patara, with its excellent harbour, at the southwest point of Lycia. Here the travellers found a ship bound for Phoenicia, which they boarded. This was an ocean going vessel, unlike the coaster they had been using, and without the hazards of an archipelago it could sail through the night. The distance from Patara to Tyre was 410 miles (660 km) and assuming the northwesterly still blew the ship may have run before the wind at seven or eight knots, covering the distance in two or three days. The delay caused by the change of plan to travel through Macedonia, and the seven days spent in Troas, probably waiting for a suitable ship, meant the travellers were too late to celebrate the Passover. However they were ahead of time to be in Jerusalem for the day of Pentecost (Acts 20: 16). This meant they could stay in Tyre seven days. But first they had to find the disciples, no simple matter in a large, commercial city.

Cyprus
During this voyage they sailed past Cyprus, leaving it on the left hand (Acts 21: 3) and no doubt Paul groaned inwardly as he was reminded of Barnabas and Mark.

After leaving Miletus Paul and his companions would have sailed past the island of Patmos, where the apostle John was later exiled.

From Tyre Paul and his companions were set on their way by the whole assembly, including wives and children. They sailed down the Galilean coast to the ancient Phoenician city of Ptolemais, where they stayed one day with the brethren, having completed the voyage. It seems the next day's journey, to Caesarea, was by land, about 35 miles (56 km) along the coastal route, passing Mount Carmel where Elijah confounded the prophets of Baal. When staying with Philip the evangelist at Caesarea the prophet Agabus accurately predicted Paul's deliverance into the hands of the Gentiles, giving emphasis to his prophecy by a dramatic enactment of bondage. This did not deter Paul from his commitment, and the next day they proceeded to Jerusalem, an uphill journey of 62 miles (100 km), accompanied by some from Caesarea, and by their future host, Mnason. He was one of the small minority of Hellenists still remaining in the Jerusalem assembly.

Ptolemais (modern Acco) where Paul and his company completed their voyage (Acts 21: 7).

So the historic journey ended. Paul went up to Jerusalem out of the conviction of his heart, his love for his people and his desire to promote unity between Jewish and Gentile believers overriding, for the moment, his commission under Christ to carry the gospel westward, to Rome and Spain. Two warnings from the Holy Spirit (Acts 21: 4, 11) confirmed his premonition that he was going into danger, yet he was fully prepared to suffer bonds and imprisonment in the city where his Master had suffered. But the visit was to lead to his arrest, and meant the end of his freedom.

SECTION 4

THE PRISON YEARS

13

PAUL'S ARREST

Paul's final visit to Jerusalem coincided with a tense political situation in Judea. After Herod Agrippa died the government of the province reverted to rule by Procurators, much to the disgust of the Jews. Under the third Procurator, Ventidius Cumanus, relations with the Jews deteriorated and a soldier caused a riot when he made an insulting gesture in the temple precincts during Passover. Troops were sent in and thousands were crushed to death in the ensuing confusion. Cumanus was succeeded by Antonius Felix, who was a freedman (ex slave), of Antonia, the mother of Emperor Claudius. His brother, Marcus Antonius Pallas, became principal financial officer of the empire and after Nero succeeded Claudius in 54 AD Pallas remained a favourite of Nero's powerful mother, Agrippina the Younger. Felix therefore had direct access to the seat of power and felt confident of the imperial favour but his cruelty, licentiousness and his willingness to accept bribes led to virtual anarchy in the province. Tacitus said of him that *he indulged in every kind of cruelty and immorality, wielding a king's authority with all the instincts of a slave* (Histories, Book 2). He put down the Jewish Zealots, but tolerated the more violent *Sicarii* (assassins), and was implicated in the murder of Jonathan, the high priest who had helped to put him in office. So Paul came to a province in ferment. Lawlessness was out of control and messianic agitators exploited the instability. Only a few months before his visit one of these, an Egyptian, rallied several thousand followers to overcome the Roman garrison. He was defeated, but escaped. The chiliarch at first mistook Paul for this anarchist (Acts 21: 38).

The Jerusalem assembly

In the assembly the Hellenists (Greek speaking Jews) were now a tiny minority. It is thought Peter, John and the other apostles had left the city in the early 50s AD. This left James, the brother of the Lord, and writer of the epistle, who provided leadership. He maintained the stance of the Acts 15 letter and confirms this at Paul's final visit (Acts 21: 25). However there were also a large number of Jewish converts – Acts 21: 20 says many thousands, or many myriads – who were all zealous of the law, and not ready to accept Paul's teaching that *in Christ Jesus neither circumcision has any force, nor uncircumcision; but faith working through love* (Galatians 5: 6). There were also those who flatly opposed Gentiles being received without their being circumcised. Such were enemies of Paul's glad tidings, operating to undermine the Gentile assemblies he had established, and it shows the apostle's indomitable courage that he was prepared to go to the very centre of Judaism to confront these persons that he knew were vehemently against him.

James

James, brother of the Lord, known as *James the Just* on account of his righteousness, was the leader in the Jerusalem assembly, and writer of the epistle in his name. He was martyred, according to the historian Josephus, before the siege of Jerusalem in 70 AD. Summoned to appear before the High Priest, he was called on to renounce his belief in the divinity of Christ, and after making a bold declaration of his faith was condemned to death and hurled from a pinnacle of the temple. Josephus regarded the destruction of Jerusalem in 70 AD as retribution for the murder of James.

The day after Paul's arrival James and the elders heard his systematic account of the work among the Gentiles, and glorified God. However their main concern was to placate the Jewish converts, and their apparent lack of appreciation of Paul's distinctiveness is betrayed in the slightly condescending way they addressed him – *Thou seest, brother* (Acts 21: 20). They then came up with a proposal to pre-empt a conflict that seemed about to erupt concerning Paul's reported views on circumcision. Paul was to finance four Nazarites who had taken a vow, and be purified with them. This would convince the doubters that there was no question of him not keeping the law. Paul, prepared to go to any lengths to bring in healing, submitted to this strategy. The next day he was purified with the men, and entered the temple.

Notices in Greek warned that any Gentile who crossed the barrier between the court of the Gentiles and the sanctuary would have only himself to blame for his ensuing death. A translation reads as follows:

No foreigner is to pass within the railing and enclosure around the temple; whosoever may be caught will be responsible to himself that death is the result.

The riot in the temple

The outer court of the temple, the Court of the Gentiles, was the limit of access to non-Jews. Notices carved on stone in Greek forbade Gentiles to cross the low stone balustrade that enclosed the inner court, and warned of the death penalty for trespassers. This barrier was *the middle wall of enclosure* referred to in Ephesians 2: 14. When he rebuilt the temple Herod enlarged the outer court to some thirty-five acres and extended it up to his Antonia fortress, at the north western corner, which he named after Mark Antony. This fortress, to the humiliation of the Jews, dominated the temple court. As well as barracks and courtyards it contained luxury accommodation for the Procurator when he visited. Staircases gave rapid access to the temple, and to the roof of the cloisters. At this time the fortress was garrisoned by a cohort of around one thousand men, seven hundred and sixty foot soldiers and two hundred and forty cavalry. They were under the command of a tribune (chiliarch).

A model of Antonia fortress, Jerusalem, in the second temple period.

All went well until near the end of the seven day period when Jews from Asia recognised Paul in the temple. They seized him and raised an outcry, accusing him of subverting Jewish teachings, and bringing Greeks into the inner court. They had seen Paul in the city with Trophimus the Ephesian and wrongly assumed that Trophimus had been brought into the area of the temple that was forbidden to Gentiles.

The Jews were in such a state of tension that an accusation of this nature acted like a spark on petrol. The crowds erupted in fury. Paul was dragged out of the Temple and the enormous gates swung slowly shut. The angry mob set on Paul to kill him and his life was only spared by the sudden appearance of the Roman chiliarch, with centurions and soldiers, who rushed down the steps from the fortress on being told of the tumult. The chiliarch, receiving no clear answer to his enquiries, commanded Paul to be brought into the fortress. But pressure from the mob forced the soldiers, bearing Paul, up the staircase, the Jews shouting *Away with him* – the very same cry used against Christ (Luke 23: 18). The chiliarch, astonished by Paul's courteous request, in fluent Greek, for permission to speak to him began to realise he was dealing with no ordinary prisoner, and certainly not with the Egyptian leader of the assassins. He granted Paul permission to address the crowd and the apostle stood on the steps and beckoned with his hand to the people. It shows his extraordinary personality that the crowd, which a minute previously would have torn him apart, fell into a profound silence.

It was a dramatic scene: the ornate temple buildings; the grim towers of the fortress; the great apostle, in chains and surrounded by Roman soldiers; the frenzied crowd below, filled with latent anger but restrained, for the moment, as Paul addressed them in Aramaic. They heard him out while he simply recounted his conversion, stressing the impeccable Jewish credentials of Ananias. But when he related the Lord's intention to send him to the nations afar off their anger broke forth anew. The reference to the nations acted like a hair trigger and all the depth of prejudice of Jew against Gentile erupted in an explosion of hatred, with its ferocity concentrated on the apostle. The chiliarch, mystified as to the cause of the Jews' malevolence, ordered Paul to be brought into the fortress and examined by scourging to find out what he had done to arouse such passions.

Scourging was a callous Roman torture to make a prisoner confess his crimes. However, Paul's calm enquiry as to the legality of scourging a Roman brought the proceedings to an abrupt halt. Valerian and Porcian laws protected the rights of Roman citizens, and the cry *civis Romanus sum* saved many an alleged miscreant from degrading punishment. Paul was no miscreant, nor had he paid a large bribe, like the chiliarch, to obtain Roman citizenship, but had inherited it from his father. Claudius Lysias was now afraid. By putting Paul in chains and preparing him for scourging the chiliarch had flagrantly violated the law.

The Sanhedrim, before whom Paul appeared the next day, assembled in the same *Gazith* Hall of Meeting on the south side of the temple where Stephen had spoken some twenty-five years before. On that occasion Paul had been an accuser. Now he stood before them as a defendant, a man who had once been one of them, and knew more of the law and the Scriptures than any of them, but had renounced Judaism utterly in the service of Christ after the greatest conversion ever. In fact he had taken up Stephen's testimony and carried it forward.

The apostle took the initiative in a bold statement of his good conscience with God, but the high priest, Ananias, who was evidently not recognisable by his clothing, commanded him to be smitten. He was known for his cruelty and injustice and according to Josephus he purloined meat from the temple sacrifices, like Eli's sons, and took illegal tithes from the threshing floors. Paul's reply, whatever its intended meaning, was prophetically fulfilled when Ananias was killed by the *Sicarri* (assassins) in 66 AD. Still retaining the initiative, as always, Paul then cried out that he was a Pharisee, which caused instant tumult. The scribes of the Pharisees started to defend him, accepting that he may have seen a vision. The Sanhedrim descended into chaos and the chiliarch was forced to intervene, sending in soldiers to save Paul's life.

Paul was returned to the fortress and it may have seemed that his visit to Jerusalem could hardly have turned out worse. However the Lord's personal appearing to encourage him, and assure him that he would bear witness at Rome, freed him from the torment of doubt and showed that all was under divine control.

A journey at night, on horseback

The degradation of the chief priests and elders was seen in their apparent willingness to agree to the illegal plot to murder Paul. His sister's son acted promptly and wisely in reporting it to the apostle, although he took his life in his hands by doing so. The chiliarch, Claudius Lysias, on being told of the conspiracy decided to move his prisoner that night to Caesarea. In his letter to Felix he claimed he rescued Paul because he found out he was a Roman, and discreetly omitted to mention that he was on the point of scourging him without a trial. The large escort for just one prisoner may seem excessive, but this was a lawless province. The chiliarch was well aware of the vehemence of the Jews, and knew they would stop at nothing. That night the troop clattered out of Jerusalem three hours after sunset taking the road to Antipatris, at the foot of the Judaean hills, a distance of about 35 miles (56 km). The way led north along a 2,500 foot (762 metres) high ridge of the mountains to Gophna, then northwest, steadily descending through Thamna, down to the coastal plain and on to Antipatris. The next day the horsemen took Paul, who had been provided with a relay of mounts, on to Caesarea, a further 27 miles (43 km). Here Felix, after learning he was from Cilicia, consigned him to Herod's praetorium. Cilicia was probably not a province at this time, otherwise Felix might have ordered the case to be heard there.

But the following night the Lord stood by him, and said, Be of good courage; for as thou hast testified the things concerning me at Jerusalem, so thou must bear witness at Rome also.

Acts 23: 11

Jerusalem to Caesarea
62 miles (100 km)

CHAPTER 14

"PRISONER OF JESUS CHRIST"

The imprisonment of Paul ended his public ministry, at least so far as Luke's account is concerned. However all was under divine control. Whatever the circumstances of his going up to Jerusalem, the apostle's final visit there was necessary to bring out the totality of the Jews' rejection of grace. His being taken to Rome as a prisoner became the means of testimony, even to the emperor himself. And the prison epistles, of such value to the church, resulted from his detention.

Caesarea, where Paul was imprisoned, was the political and commercial capital of Judea, just as Jerusalem was the religious centre. It was a new town, developed by Herod into a Hellenistic city with a theatre and amphitheatre. Its port was the main point of entry or departure for the province.

After Herod Agrippa I died in 44 AD and direct Roman rule was resumed in Judea, tensions between the Jews and their governors increased, and

the prison epistles
The epistles written by Paul when he was a prisoner are Ephesians, Philippians, Colossians, Philemon and the second letter to Timothy. It is possible he also wrote the epistle to the Hebrews during his confinement. The second letter to Timothy was evidently written shortly before Paul's martyrdom, possibly after he had been re-arrested.

The entrance to the harbour at Caesarea, where Paul was held as a prisoner, without charge, for two years.

eventually erupted in the Jewish revolt of 66 AD. During their terms of office Felix and Festus made futile attempts to placate the Jews by keeping Paul confined. He was imprisoned at Caesarea for over two years with no charges made against him by the Romans, in contravention of basic principles of justice, for reasons that were entirely political. Under Roman law cases had to be heard quickly, but there was no time limit for conducting a trial once proceedings had begun.

However Luke is writing in the Acts to bring out that Paul was free from any wrongdoing, just as he also records three times in his gospel that Pilate found nothing in Jesus that could be condemned (Luke 23: 4, 14, 15 and 22). He notes that Claudius Lysias found no charge which would justify imprisonment or death (Acts 23: 29). He records that Festus and Agrippa reach a similar conclusion

Looking north along the top of a high level aqueduct built by Herod the Great to supply water to Caesarea.

(Acts 26: 31). Finally he describes how Paul is allowed to preach and teach freely in the capital of the empire (Acts 28: 31). This clearly demonstrated that the Roman authorities, during the period covered by the Acts, had no issue with Paul or his service, and were not moving to proscribe Christianity.

The hearing before Felix

The flattering style of address adopted by Tertullus, the advocate of the Jews, was the convention at hearings of this nature. There was, however, rich irony in saying *we enjoy great peace* when the province was in near anarchy. It was also untrue to say they would have judged Paul according to their law had not Lysias intervened when in fact they were trying to kill him without a trial. Tertullus accused Paul of moving sedition; leading a sect, which implied heresy; and profaning the temple, which offended both Jewish and Roman law.

Paul's shining manliness and honesty contrasted with the sophistry of his accusers. His defence exposed the falseness of their charges. He had committed no wrong. His conduct at Jerusalem had been impeccable. He believed the law and prophets. And he had hope in a resurrection, as they did. He also drew attention to the absence of the Jews from Asia, who had made the original charge. Felix was married to a Jewess, Drusilla, and knew enough about the Jews and the Christian way to see where the truth lay. But rather than offend the Jews, and lacking the moral courage to make a right judgement he opted for adjournment. However he gave his prisoner a degree of liberty, and allowed his friends to see him. It appears Paul was under military arrest, *custodia militaris*, which involved being chained to a soldier. This seems to be confirmed by Acts 24: 27, Acts 26: 29 and other scriptures.

The new faith of Christianity was attracting general attention at this time, and beginning to be widely known. Felix and Drusilla, his second wife, were interested to know more so Paul was sent for and given an opportunity to testify. Drusilla, a Jewess, was at this time around twenty-two years old. She had originally been the wife of Azizus, king of Emasa, who submitted to circumcision in order to marry her. Felix, overcome by her beauty, had employed a Jewish friend, masquerading as a magician, to persuade her to abandon her husband and transgress the Jewish law in order to become his wife, although he was a Gentile. She was daughter of Agrippa the first, and sister of Agrippa and Bernice, who would shortly hear Paul's defence. Felix was quite unprepared for Paul's direct appeal to his conscience in the subsequent interview. The idea of judgement to come brought fear into his soul, and he found an excuse to dismiss the one person who could have shown him and his wife the way of salvation. He kept sending for Paul, however, hoping the apostle would buy his freedom with a bribe. In this he was mistaken.

During Felix's term of office a conflict arose between the Syrian and Jewish citizens of Caesarea. Felix was accused by the Jews and kept Paul imprisoned in a last attempt to gain their favour. This proved unavailing and he was recalled by Nero, but escaped unpunished due to the influence of his brother Pallas.

The hearing before Festus

Porcius Festus succeeded Felix. When he visited Jerusalem the Jews, their hatred still burning against Paul, begged him to send the apostle to them, ostensibly for trial but in fact so they could murder him. Instead, Festus arranged a hearing at Caesarea. The Jews accused, and once again were unable to make good their charges. Festus wanted the Jews to support him so allowed politics to eclipse justice. He was content to use Paul as a pawn in the political game if it would help his own career. So he proposed a trial at Jerusalem. Paul, with dignity, pointed out the unfairness of this when there was not a single substantiated charge, and then, in an unexpected move, appealed to Caesar. *Caesarem apello* was a cry open to any Roman citizen in any part of the empire, and one Festus had no choice but to allow. Although there was a possibility Paul would have been released had he not appealed to Caesar, which was confirmed by Agrippa in Acts 26: 32, a hearing before the emperor was preferable to one at Jerusalem. Paul later told the Roman Jews that he was *compelled* to appeal to Caesar (Acts 28: 19). He evidently saw no alternative.

The right of appeal – *provocatio* – to the emperor developed from the right of appeal to the Roman people, the *populous Romanus*, which was one of the most ancient rights of a Roman citizen. It went back to the foundation of the Republic in 509 BC. Usually exercised against a magistrate's verdict, it could be used at any point in a trial. During the *quinquennium Neronis*, the first five years of Nero's rule from 54 to 59 AD, the administration of the empire was under the influence of Seneca, Nero's teacher, a Stoic philosopher, and Sextus Afranius Burrus, prefect of the Praetorian Guard. This was remembered as a golden age, and the later excesses of this emperor were held in check. So an appeal to the emperor at this time would have had a reasonable chance of being heard fairly.

The appeal left Festus in a difficult position. He would now have to prepare a report for the emperor about a case where there were no charges, and involving issues he could hardly understand. The arrival of Agrippa and Bernice, to congratulate Festus on his new appointment, offered a way out. He outlined the case to Agrippa, taking care to present himself in the best light, and Agrippa expressed the desire to hear Paul.

Julius Agrippa was the last of the House of Herod. His father, Agrippa I, had beheaded James the apostle. His great grandfather had slaughtered the infant boys in Bethlehem. And his great uncle Antipas had murdered John the Baptist. When his father died ignominiously at Caesarea (Acts 12: 23) the emperor, Claudius, was inclined to appoint the young Agrippa as his successor. He was dissuaded, however, since Agrippa was only seventeen. So Judea reverted to rule by procurators. Instead, on the death of Herod, his uncle, he was given the kingdom of Chalcis (Lebanon). Later he received

Bronze coin of Herod Agrippa I, father of Agrippa in Acts 26.

the tetrarchies of Philip and Lysanias, referred to in Luke 3: 1. Nero further added various cities of Galilee. Julia Bernice, his sister, had married her uncle, Herod, king of Chalcis. After he died she lived in the house of her brother Agrippa, apart from a brief second marriage to Polemo, king of Cilicia. The relationship between Agrippa and Bernice was widely regarded as incestuous. On state occasions Agrippa treated her as his queen. Subsequently she formed a relationship with Titus, the future emperor. The Herods were Edomites, but followed the Jewish faith, and Agrippa at this time had the authority to appoint the high priests. So he was not only well informed about religious questions, but also curious to know more about Christianity, in which there was considerable interest everywhere.

The hearing before Agrippa

Paul's examination by Agrippa was an unofficial enquiry at the invitation of Festus, who wanted something to write to the emperor about Paul. It was not a trial, which Agrippa had no authority to conduct in Judea, but a semi-formal occasion attended by military officers and the chief men of Caesarea. Paul stretched out his hand when invited to speak: he was evidently still bound (Acts 26: 29) probably by his right hand to a soldier's left. But although in chains Paul was the freest man in the court, in contrast to Agrippa and Bernice whose lives bore witness to the bondage of their degradation.

The apostle's clear account of his life brought out his impeccable Jewish background, his hope in the fulfilment of prophecies, his persecution of Christians, his conversion, and his subsequent service which was the reason for the Jews' antagonism. His defence was interrupted by an outburst from Festus, whose mask of politeness had now slipped, denouncing him as mad. But Paul's calm answer showed he was in perfect control of his faculties, and he went on to make a direct appeal to Agrippa's conscience. The king was not ready for this and embarrassed at being put in such a position by a prisoner he attempted to turn the question with a jest. Paul's wonderful reply would include everyone present in his own peace and happiness, which were undaunted after two years in prison. He was totally superior to the situation. Agrippa's conscience, however, had been reached. In the subsequent consultation both he and Festus agreed that Paul was innocent of any crime. This was an important point, especially since Luke's account would be used to influence persons in high places about the character of Christianity. We have no record whether or not the Jerusalem assembly attempted to provide support for Paul in all these hearings.

the Roman army

The Roman Empire was built on its military strength and the Roman army was the first in the world to use full time, paid soldiers. In the time of Augustus there were some 28 legions, each commanded by a Legate and consisting of around 5,500 soldiers. Every legion was made up from a first cohort of 800 men with specialist skills, nine cohorts of 480 men divided into six centuries of approximately 80 men each, and a cavalry division of 120 men, used mainly as scouts. A cohort was a division of 480 (or 800) men, commanded by a tribune (Greek *chiliarch*) and made up of centuries. A century was the smallest division in the Roman army, commanded by a centurion. Originally a century consisted of 100 men but this was later reduced to 80 men. Legates and tribunes would usually be Roman citizens, drawn from the equestrian (middle) class, intent on a career in public service. All soldiers, however, would be given Roman citizenship after completing twenty-five years of service. The term *Praetorium* (Acts 23: 35, Philippians 1: 13) originally meant the tent of a commander (*Praetor*) and became a word used to describe the army headquarters.

THE SHIPWRECK

Luke is again writing as an eyewitness (from Acts 27: 1) and many studies have proved the accuracy of his vivid narrative, his knowledge of the sea being evidenced in his unerring use of nautical terms. Aristarchus, a Macedonian from Thessalonica, who had been with Paul at Ephesus, accompanied Paul on the voyage. He may also have been a prisoner: Paul later calls him *my fellow-captive* (Colossians 4: 10).

Paul was under the custody of Julius, a centurion of Augustus' company, which may have been one of the five cohorts stationed in Judea, or possibly a cohort of the Praetorian Guard. By the end of the voyage he had begun to realise the distinctiveness of his prisoner but even at Sidon, the first port of call, he treated Paul kindly and allowed him to visit his friends. Some have identified him with Julius Priscus who was later prefect of the Praetorian guards, under the emperor, Vitellius. The other wretched prisoners in his charge were probably being shipped to the capital so they could die in Roman arenas, providing hideous spectacles of bloodshed for entertainment.

Unfavourable winds

The ship Paul sailed in as far as Myra was from Adramyttium, a port in the eastern Aegean Sea, southeast of Troas. She was probably a coasting vessel, on her way back to her base, and the centurion's intention was to tranship at an Asian port. To avoid strong westerly winds they turned north and sailed under the lee of Cyprus, along the north shore, where they would also have been helped by smooth water, westward currents, and winds blowing offshore from Cilicia. So they arrived at Myra in Lycia, and here Julius encountered a merchant ship from Alexandria, bound for Italy, which they boarded. He must have

The harbour at Myra (modern Kale) where the centurion and his prisoners transferred to a grain ship bound for Rome (Acts 27: 6).

been pleased to find a ship sailing for Rome so late in the season. The alternative would have been a coastal ship to Troas and Neapolis, and a land journey to the Adriatic. Ships from Alexandria bound for Rome often went north, and then along the Asian coast, to avoid unfavourable winds. A typical voyage time from Alexandria to Puteoli, the port for Rome, was fifteen to twenty days. Pliny the Elder records a voyage in the reverse direction, with a following wind, that took only nine days.

The new vessel was a grain ship (see chapter 2) and from Myra she battled along the Asian coast in the face of a north-westerly wind, as far as the point of Cnidus, *which took many days*, although the distance was only about 150 miles (241 km). Ancient ships could sail no closer to the wind than about seven points, and relied on a large square mainsail, which limited the degree to which they could tack. After Cnidus they lost the advantage of a weather shore, and a favourable current, and could evidently make no headway. So they turned south, passing Salmone, the eastern point of Crete, and then sailing west along the south shore of the island. Here they were again heading into the northwest wind, but with the advantage of a weather shore, and were able to reach Fair Havens, the last harbour before Cape Matala, where the coast turns suddenly north. This was as far as they could go in such wind conditions.

Paul counselled they should stay in this harbour at Fair Havens, Crete, for the winter, but his advice was not heeded (Acts 27: 10, 11).

Paul's advice is refused

The voyage so far had taken much longer than expected, and *the fast was already past* – a reference to the Jewish Day of Atonement which fell in late September or early October. The safe sailing season was reckoned by the Romans from the fifth day of the Ides of March to the third of the Ides of November. The restriction was not only on account of bad weather: there were no compasses – they were scarcely known in Europe before the twelfth century – so if skies were overcast sailors could not navigate. It was clearly not going to be possible to complete the voyage in the present season, so the question was whether they should winter at Fair Havens, or go on to Phoenice, modern Lutra, further along the coast.

Paul's counsel was very definite. He predicted disaster and loss of cargo, ship and lives if they sailed on. But the helmsman and shipowner thought they should take the chance. Phoenice was only 45 miles (72 km) away, and had a sheltered harbour, whereas Fair Havens was more exposed. Julius was swayed by their arguments, but their advice was flawed. Although open, the harbour at Fair Havens was partly protected by islands, and sailing to Phoenice involved real risk of being driven off to sea in an unexpected gale – which is exactly what happened. Paul was right, as events proved.

Julius the centurion
It was Julius, the centurion, who made the final decision to sail on from Fair Havens. As a servant of the empire he would have carried an official pass, *diplomata*, which empowered him to compel civilians, including captains of sailing ships, to assist him (as Matthew 5: 41 *And whoever will compel thee to go one mile, go with him two*).

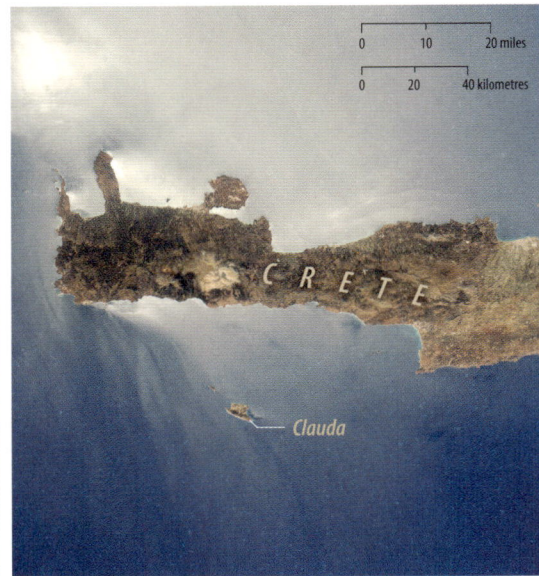

This view from the island of Clauda looks towards the snow-capped hills of Crete about 30 miles (48 km) away, and gives an idea of the distance Paul's ship was blown, out of control, by the hurricane. This tiny island which provided brief respite is today called Gavdos and has about forty inhabitants. Its scale in relation to Crete is clear from the satellite image on the right.

A change of wind to the south seemed ideal, and they set sail, keeping close to the coast, and believing they were as good as there. The hurricane *Euroclydon* which then struck them came suddenly from east-northeast, blasting down from Crete's 7,000 foot (2,134 metres) high mountains, and they were driven before it, unable to bring the ship's head to the wind. This was a frightening and dangerous experience with the great vessel virtually out of control and liable to be swamped by seas breaking over the stern. The distance they were driven to Clauda was about 40 miles (64 km). It is only a tiny island about seven by three miles (11 x 5 km) and if they had missed it there was nothing to stop them being blown all the way to the African coast, and the dreaded quicksands of Syrtis. In addition there was the question of damage to the ship. The violence of the hurricane on the large, square sail would exert great leverage on the single mast, straining the hull and causing the timbers to open. The consequent leaks seem to have worsened during the voyage. This would have caused the grain cargo to swell, exerting pressure on the hull, so it was partly jettisoned after leaving Clauda, and again when approaching Malta.

In the lee of Clauda they managed, with difficulty, to get the longboat on board, which had been trailing behind but was now their only hope of escape if the ship foundered. Doubtless it had taken on water. They then frapped the ship, which involved passing cables around the hull to tighten the timbers and reduce leakage. They also lowered the gear, which was probably the heavy yard and rigging of the mainsail. It appears as if Luke lent a hand in these operations. As a passenger, or possibly an attendant upon Paul, he was no doubt pressed into service or volunteered. At some stage they must have got the ship round as close to the wind as they could, probably pointing due north. An east-northeast wind on the starboard tack, with a small storm sail, set them on a drift heading approximately eight degrees north of west, which is the exact bearing of Malta from Clauda. Acts 27: 40 confirms they had a foresail. During the next two days they lightened the ship by jettisoning some of the cargo, and the furniture, which would reduce the risk of sinking.

For many days they drifted in this manner, with no idea of where they were heading, since they could not see the sun or stars, and with the storm unabated. If the leaks were increasing, as is probable, it seemed obvious the voyage could only end in one way. No one had eaten for a long time, and everyone had given up hope. At this lowest point Paul addressed them, telling them of his revelation that all were going to be saved. The effect on morale must have been great, but this was not ordinary leadership: God was ensuring that His servant would be recognised, and his words respected.

... in the end all hope of our being saved was taken away.
Acts 27: 20

Caesarea to Malta
1,550 miles (2,494 km)

An aerial view of St Paul's Bay, Malta, which has been identified as a possible site for the shipwreck since it is one of the few large sandy bays on the east coast of the island. The two small islands in the centre of the picture are known as St Paul's Islands, and the ship may have run aground just north of these (to the left, in the picture).

Winter in Malta

Luke's account of the landing at Malta cannot be improved upon. The location of St Paul's Bay, as it is called, is said to meet all the criteria in his account, including the depth of the soundings, and the local clay in the seabed which gave secure anchorage even in a storm. The distance from Clauda to the point of Koura, at Malta, is 560 miles (901 km) so that with a rate of drift of 1.6 miles per hour, which experts have said would be expected in the circumstances, the voyage would have taken fourteen or fifteen days, which agrees closely with Luke's account. Had the direction of drift varied by even a small amount Malta would have been missed, and the ship lost. To anchor from the stern was unusual but ensured the vessel was kept before the wind so that it could be run aground without having to be turned. Paul's service in pre-empting the escape of the sailors saved the lives of all, since no-one else would have been able to bring the ship to land. However the soldiers' decisive action meant they were without the benefit of the lifeboat at the one time it would have been of value. Paul then encouraged them and persuaded all to take food, setting the example himself. The words *taken a loaf*; *gave thanks*; and *broken it* are reminiscent of Luke's account of the Lord's Supper.

Thus all got safe to land. The owner and crew had lost everything through not listening to Paul, escaping only with their lives. Every human contrivance to save themselves and the ship had failed. Deliverance came from the God who controls the wind and seas, so that His servant would be honoured. By the end of the voyage everyone had been brought round to recognise Paul as the means of their salvation, and respect his nearness to God.

"AND THUS WE WENT TO ROME"

Malta was first colonised by the Phoenicians, then came under Greek rule before being brought under Roman control in 218 BC during the Carthaginian war. After that it was administered as part of the province of Sicily. The designation *Barbarians* was applied to all nations not of Greek or Roman descent, and speaking a foreign language: it does not imply they were uncivilised. The islanders most probably spoke pidgin Greek, or a form of Phoenician, and at the time of Paul's visit they were prosperous traders, especially in textiles. Paul and his company were received kindly, and blessing and healing followed. The apostle set himself to serve the father of Publius, and all the islanders, who responded with gifts to replace the essentials that had been lost in the shipwreck. It is noteworthy that the island that received Paul, and whose inhabitants were grateful for his ministrations, was protected from invasion, against all odds, during the Second World War. Some centuries earlier, in September 1565, Paul's Bay was the location for the final battle in the Great Siege of Malta, when the Ottoman forces were finally driven from the island.

After three months the party boarded an Alexandrian ship, possibly another corn trader, which had wintered in the island and had the *Dioscuri* for its ensign. Ships took their names from their figureheads, in this case Castor and Pollux, mythical protectors of sailors. They probably embarked in February, the captain hoping to get to Rome when prices in the grain market were high, after the winter. Syracuse, where they remained three days, no doubt because the wind failed them, was the principal city in Sicily and became a Roman colony under Augustus. They sailed, evidently against the wind, to Rhegium, on the Italian side of the straits

Syracuse, Sicily, where Paul stayed for three days (Acts 28: 12).

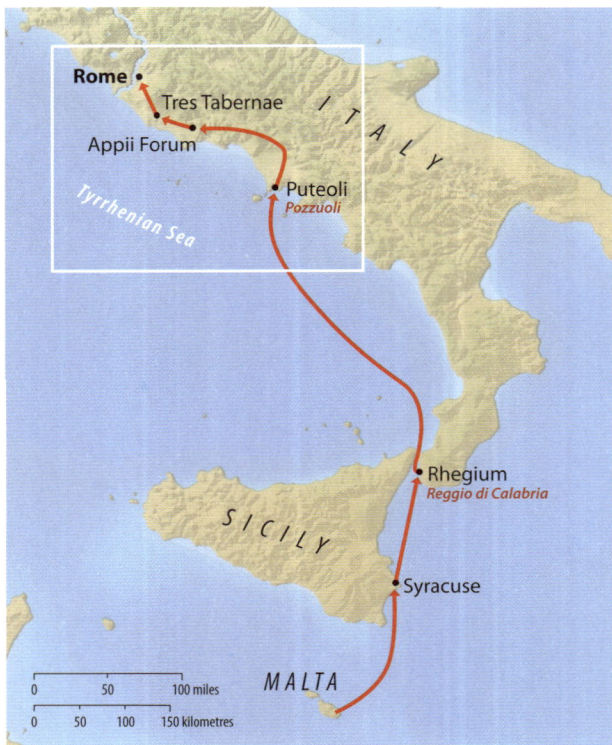

of Messina, where they waited for one day. The wind now changed, and with a southerly filling the large, square sail they negotiated the hazardous current between the rocks of Charybdis and Scylla and sailed up the coast to reach the scenic Bay of Naples, dominated by Vesuvius. Puteoli with its safe harbour, was reached on the *second day*. It was the principal port for Rome before Ostia, at the mouth of the Tiber, developed under Claudius. Seneca has described how the entire population would turn out to watch the arrival of the first grain ships of the season, the only vessels allowed to approach the port with their topsails set. This was a run of 210 miles (338 km) from Rhegium: if the speed was seven knots that would take just 26 hours. The presence of an assembly in Puteoli shows how Christianity had spread, apparently without the help of any apostles. Hebrews 13: 24 is a further reference to brethren in Italy.

The remainder of the journey to Rome was by land, a distance of 140 miles (225 km). The party would join the *Via Appia* at Capua, to the north east, or possibly at Sinuessa if they followed the coastal route. The *Via Appia* was one of the earliest and most important roads of the ancient

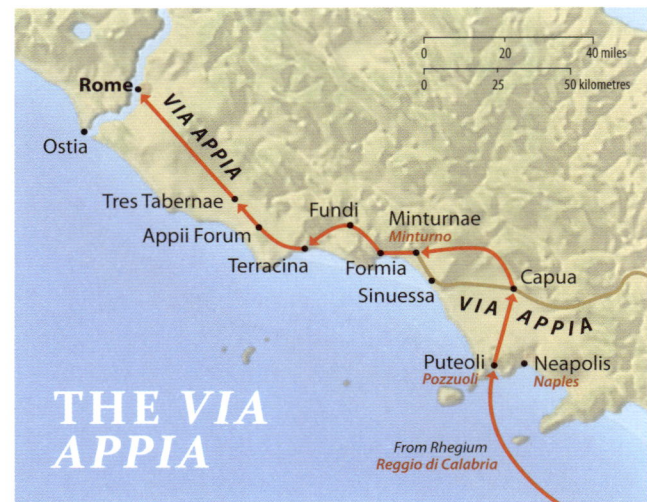

THE *VIA APPIA*

Republic, connecting Rome to Brundisium, in south east Italy, and still contains the longest section of straight highway in Europe, a span of 39 miles (63 km). The brethren from Rome, no doubt having been informed by those at Puteoli, came out to meet them at Appii Forum and Tres Tabernae, which were, respectively, 40 and 30 miles (64 and 48 km) from the city. This was a moving moment for Paul, from which he took courage.

The Appian Way: every step Paul was taken along this ancient highway brought him nearer to imprisonment at Rome.

The beach at Puteoli (modern Pozzuoli) where Paul landed and found brethren (Acts 28: 14).

The capital of the empire at that time was an immense city with a population of more than one million. Rome sprawled over its seven hills to cover an area of 6 square miles (15.5 sq km) and was encircled by 13 miles (21 km) of walls. The centurion handed over his prisoners to the praetorian prefect, the commanding officer of the emperor's bodyguard, who at this time was Afranius Burrus, advisor to the emperor, and a powerful figure in the early years of Nero's reign. Paul, however, was given *libera custodia*: he was permitted to stay in lodgings of his own, where he could receive visitors but remained lightly chained to a soldier (Acts 28: 16, 20).

Malta to Rome

520 miles (837 km)

So Paul was found in Rome, after thousands of miles of travel, and having endured untold sufferings and opposition. He had intended to come there as an evangelist, on his way to Spain. Now he was a prisoner, but according to the will of God, so that he should fulfil the Lord's commission *to bear my name before both nations and kings and the sons of Israel* (Acts 9: 15).

How would the apostle have appeared after his ordeals? The indelible scars from the scourgings he had received, and the marks from the stoning at Lystra bore testimony to the ownership of Christ, the signature of his Master. What he suffered was unique, after Christ, but his physical and mental health were preserved to the end.

A final appeal to the Jews

Paul then made his final appeal to the Jews, whom he still regarded as his own people, and as the people of God. There were said to have been seven synagogues in Rome at this time, and a Jewish population of sixty thousand. The testimony of grace had been prolonged through the intercession of Christ on the cross, but without effect. Paul pronounced judgement on the unbelieving nation, quoting the words of Isaiah's prophecy eight hundred years earlier. Luke's account ends with Paul receiving all who came to him, and teaching and preaching freely in the capital of the empire. In recording this he demonstrates to his readers in high places that Christianity was not viewed adversely by the Roman authorities.

And some were persuaded of the things which were said, but some disbelieved.

Acts 28: 24

17

THE FINAL YEARS

At the end of his life Paul was a prisoner, aged as a result of incessant service night and day for more than a quarter of a century, worn with suffering and rejected by some of his one-time followers. Yet God so overruled that these final years in captivity were a fitting climax to the apostle's service. Firstly, the Lord had assured him he would bear witness at Rome (Acts 23: 11) and there can be no doubt that this happened. Paul's imprisonment made the gospel known in the high places of the capital of the empire and he rendered a testimony to the greatest personages in the world at that time, doubtless to the emperor himself. Secondly, the written words of Paul in his prison epistles have affected many more millions of souls than he was allowed to preach to in his lifetime, and reached down the ages to the present time. What seemed a great victory to the enemy in the imprisonment of the apostle was turned by God to spread the gospel.

Why did Luke finish his account so abruptly, without recounting the apostle's final years? Some think he may have intended to write a third account, detailing later events. Others speculate that he died, or was martyred. But the important point is that Luke ends the Acts with Paul able to preach freely, and Christianity clearly a religion permitted by the Roman Empire. Having established this point Luke may have regarded subsequent events as not relevant to his discourse.

Paul's companions at Rome

The presence of loyal brethren must have made all the difference to Paul's confinement. Aristarchus of Thessalonica who had sailed with Paul from Caesarea was still with him at Rome when he wrote to the Colossians and Paul refers to him as *my fellow-captive* (4: 10). Timothy is included in the salutations in Paul's letters to the Philippians, to the Colossians and to Philemon. Later he was apparently sent away in service: Paul's second letter to him urges his return without delay (2 Timothy 4: 9, 11, 21). Epaphroditus came from Macedonia bearing gifts from the Philippians: he was *sick close*

to death (Philippians 2: 27) whilst in the capital. Tychicus, from Asia, was entrusted with the letters for Ephesus and Colosse and returned to Asia with Onesimus. Later Paul told Timothy he had sent him to Ephesus (2 Timothy 4: 12), and tells Titus that he may send him to Crete. Epaphras from Colosse was with Paul in Rome and brought him news of the Colossians (Colossians 1: 7, 8 and 4: 12). Mark also appears to have been with Paul at Rome (Colossians 4: 10; Philemon 24) and in the letter to Philemon he is included as one of the apostle's *fellow workmen*.

Towards the end of his life, when the government was actively persecuting Christians, Paul had few companions, and his loneliness is evident from his second letter to Timothy. A visit from Onesiphorus during this period therefore gave the apostle great encouragement. He is commended for having sought him out very diligently (2 Timothy 1: 16–18) and he was happy to be in Paul's company, unlike many who did not want to associate with a man who was by then in disgrace with the authorities, and a prisoner. This may even have cost him his life: the second reference in 2 Timothy (4: 19) refers only to his house. We are not told where he was from, but he had rendered some service for Paul in Ephesus. Luke accompanied Paul in the shipwreck, and to Rome: some years later Paul tells Timothy that Luke was the only one still with him (2 Timothy 4: 11). It appears that none of the brethren in Rome stood with Paul at his first defence (2 Timothy 4: 16) but Eubulus, Pudens, Linus and Claudia are named in the salutations at the end of Paul's second letter to Timothy. Presumably they were brethren local at Rome, who still had contact with the apostle.

The prison epistles

The epistles written (or dictated) by Paul when he was a prisoner are Ephesians, Philippians, Colossians, Philemon and 2 Timothy. He may also have written the epistle to the Hebrews at this time.

The first four evidently belong to the earlier stage of Paul's confinement, and Philippians was probably written first. The brethren from Philippi had sent Epaphroditus to Rome, a journey of 800 miles (1,287 km), with gifts (Philippians 4: 18). In his letter of thanks Paul is positive about his circumstances in view of the opportunity they gave to promote the glad tidings in all the praetorium, and beyond. The brethren, despite Paul's bonds, were also preaching fearlessly (1: 12–14). The reference to Caesar's household (4: 22) is another indicator of how quickly the gospel had spread at Rome during the apostle's time there, and he seems optimistic of an early release (2: 24).

The apostle's letters to the Ephesians and Colossians were both written around the same time, and delivered by Tychicus (Ephesians 6: 21, Colossians 4: 7).

The imprisonment of Paul did not inhibit his capacity to bring in healing. Onesimus, a slave who had fled from his master, encountered Paul in Rome and the grace shown him by the apostle melted his resistance. Paul knew about bondmanship. He himself was everyone's slave, available to serve all, and now he served Onesimus to set him free and send him back to his master, Philemon, no longer as a bondman, but a beloved brother (Philemon 16). He had made a long journey from Colosse to Rome, something like 1,200 miles (1,931 km), but now he retraced his

Paul's letters
Paul wrote his letters in *Koine*, the Hellenistic Greek of his day. This was the form of Greek spoken internationally, which served as the *lingua franca* of the western world. Known as *common* Greek, it developed and spread with the conquests of Alexander the Great, and is the language of the Septuagint, and of the New Testament. Some scholars believe that the epistle to the Hebrews is an exception, and was written in Hebrew. If so, that would be consistent with the strategy of the writer to win the Hebrews by using their traditional language.

Caesar's household
The household of Caesar (Philippians 4: 22) was the equivalent of a modern civil service and included many officials who administered the empire, some of whom had evidently been converted.

steps in the company of Tychicus with a letter from Paul to his master. The apostle's request that Philemon should prepare to receive him as a guest (Philemon 22) again shows that he hoped for early release.

2 Timothy was clearly written near the end of Paul's life. If he was released the letter would have been written soon after he was re-arrested when he had already had one court hearing and was awaiting the final outcome. The government was by this time inimical to Christians: Paul, anticipating the end, appealed to Timothy to join him urgently. The epistle to the Hebrews may also have been written during this later imprisonment as indicated by the salutation *They from Italy salute you* (Hebrews 13: 24).

Timothy set at liberty
The reference in Hebrews 13: 23 to Timothy being set at liberty could possibly mean that he was arrested in Rome and then liberated, since Hebrews may have been written at this time.

The Roman government

When Paul appealed to Caesar (Acts 25: 11) Nero's government was in its early years and the disastrous flaws in his character had not yet become evident. He became emperor in 54 AD, aged 16, after the death of Claudius, who was said to have been poisoned by his wife, Agrippina, Nero's mother. Three persons exerted strong influence on the early years of Nero's reign: Agrippina; Seneca the younger, a Stoic philosopher who was tutor to Nero, and older brother of Gallio (Acts 18: 12); and Sextus Afranius Burrus, Prefect of the Praetorian Guard, to whose care Paul had been committed (Acts 28: 16). There was a tradition in the early church that Paul and Seneca became acquainted. There is no direct evidence for this, but his liberal views are believed to have promoted the relaxed Imperial policy towards other religions which allowed the spread of Christianity in Paul's day. And Burrus must have been favourably disposed to Paul after hearing from Julius how he had saved all their lives in the shipwreck. The leaders in Rome were in close relationship, and the presence of a distinguished prisoner, pioneer of the new faith of Christianity, would not go unnoticed. The influence of the apostle on the makers of policy may well have been considerable.

The Praetorian Guard was a force of bodyguards used by Roman emperors. When Paul arrived in Rome the Prefect of the Praetorian Guard was Sextus Afranius Burrus who is believed to have been favourable to Paul, and had considerable influence over Nero in the early part of his reign. He died however in 62 AD.

The situation, however, changed as Nero asserted his independence. Agrippina lost influence after she objected to an association between her son

and a former slave girl, Claudia Acte, and Nero is believed to have ordered her murder in 59 AD. Burrus died in 62 AD, some say poisoned by Nero; and Seneca was ordered to commit suicide by the emperor in 65 AD after alleged involvement in a plot against him. Ofonius Tigellinus, notorious for his cruelty and debauchery, succeeded Burrus as Prefect of the Praetorian Guard and became Nero's principal adviser from 62 to 68 AD. Also in 62 AD Nero married Poppaea Sabina, who had Jewish sympathies, after his wife, Claudia Octavia, had been executed.

It can be seen, from this sordid history, that elements in the government that might have been favourable to Paul declined as Nero's reign advanced, with the possible exception of Poppaea.

There was clearly a change of attitude towards Christians during Paul's time in Rome. At the end of Acts Paul is described as preaching and teaching freely, with no restriction from the government, yet after the fire of Rome in 64 AD Christians were perceived as an illegal sect whose members were against the state, and no longer enjoying legal protection as a branch of Judaism.

The Great Fire of Rome in 64 AD burned for some days and destroyed much of the city. According to the Roman historian Tacitus (56 AD to 117 AD) Nero blamed Christians for starting it, thus deflecting the anger of the populace from himself. With Tigellinus, his evil lieutenant, the emperor started a persecution against Christians and many were martyred with every refinement of cruelty, which may be the persecution referred to in 1 Peter 4: 12–16. This may have been when Paul was re-arrested, but it could equally be true that his re-arrest and martyrdom were before the great fire. But even if Paul had remained in Rome under arrest the whole time it would have made little difference: those favourable to him in the government, Seneca, Burrus and possibly Agrippina either died or fell out of favour so that Nero and Tigellinus ruled virtually unrestrained.

Was Paul released?

Was Paul released and then re-arrested? The tradition of the early church is united that he was, and Clement of Rome, believed to be the Clement of Philippians 4: 3, writing around 96 AD said of the apostle:

> *he taught righteousness through the whole world and having*
> *reached the limits of the west [Greek further limits] he bore*

testimony to the rulers, and so departed from the world and was
taken up into the holy place – the greatest example of endurance.
1 Clement 5: 1–7

Many think the expression the *limits of the west* indicates Spain, but it may simply refer to Rome. Early church leaders such as John Chrysostom and Jerome also assert that Paul was released, and so does the church historian, Eusebius of Caesarea, but none of this is conclusive since these persons lived in the third, fourth or fifth centuries, and must have been repeating oral tradition. And there is no tradition in the Spanish Church that links its origin to a visit from Paul.

References in Scripture to visits and journeys that are apparently not recorded in the Acts seem to confirm the probability that he was released, and undertook further service before being re-arrested, and J.N. Darby wrote:

> *It is possible that he may have been liberated; I believe so, from*
> *what we find in the Epistles to the Philippians and to Philemon;*
> *Phil. 1: 25, 26; Philemon 22.* (*Collected Writings* volume 25 page 415)

Other references mention visits to Ephesus and Macedonia (1 Timothy 1: 3); visits to Troas and Miletus (2 Timothy 4: 13, 20); an apparent visit to Crete (Titus 1: 5); and possibly a visit to Corinth (2 Timothy 4: 20). Paul also refers to spending the winter at Nicopolis (Titus 3: 12). These visits may well have taken place after Paul was released, and their absence from the Acts suggests they were perhaps subsequent to Luke's account. However it is also possible they occurred before Paul became a prisoner, for example the visit to Crete could have been during the three years he spent at Ephesus, even although it is not recorded by Luke.

Many have wondered if the apostle's apparently hurried departure from Troas, where he left his cloak, books and parchments, infers that this was where he was re-arrested, and whether Alexander the smith (2 Timothy 4: 14, 15) had any part in denouncing him, and if he did, whether he had any connection with the silver-beaters who opposed Paul at Ephesus (Acts 19: 24–28) or was the spokesman put forward by the Jews in the arena (Acts 19: 33). If Paul was indeed released from imprisonment the second letter to Timothy was clearly written after he had been re-arrested.

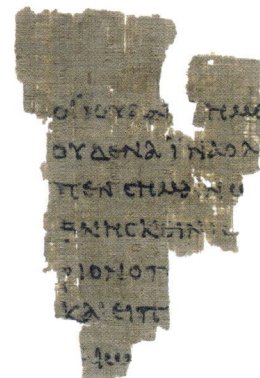

Papyrus fragment of St John's Gospel, Chapter 18, verses 31–33, in which Christ appears before Pilate. It was discovered in Upper Egypt, possibly at Oxyrhynchus. Part of a codex, it is the earliest known fragment of the New Testament in any language, and is now preserved in the John Ryland Library, Manchester, England.

Paul's second imprisonment

Paul, in his second letter to Timothy, says *I suffer even unto bonds as an evil-doer*, (2 Timothy 2: 9). So his later confinement may have been more severe and involved penal detention *custodia publica* rather than the military custody *custodia militaris* which he had been permitted during the first two years in Rome, and which allowed him to choose his own place of lodging. However the apostle was still able to receive Onesiphorus and Luke, and send letters (2 Timothy), as well as having contact with his local brethren (2 Timothy 4: 21).

There is another tradition that Paul and Peter were imprisoned together in the dreaded Mamertinum gaol, and modern visitors are shown numerous artefacts affirming their alleged confinement. However closer examination reveals that this tradition is no earlier than sixth century, and lacks any shred of supporting evidence.

The legal case against Paul

Paul was no stranger to litigation against him. At Philippi he had been accused of disturbing public order. At Thessolonica he faced the more serious charge of promoting another king, Jesus, against Caesar. At Corinth his enemies claimed he was persuading men to worship contrary to the law. After his arrest at Jerusalem the accusations outlined by Tertullus included sedition and profaning the temple. It was because Paul appealed to be heard by Caesar, rather than by the Jews in Jerusalem, that he had been brought to Rome. However a case against him depended on his accusers appearing in person within a certain time. This may be the significance of the *two whole years* at the end of Acts: if Paul's accusers had not made the long journey from Jerusalem within the legal time limit the case against him would have been dropped. If so, this may have been when the great apostle was set free for a time.

Roman laws
Roman laws against treason and sedition were reinstated in 62 AD and this was also the year in which Burrus died, Seneca was dismissed and Nero married Poppaea, a Jewess who may well have supported the Jews against Paul.

As a Roman citizen Paul enjoyed considerable legal rights, including exemption from torture, and from crucifixion. A capital charge against him could only be brought for a serious offence, and the most likely charge would be one of lese-majesty *crimen laesae maiestatis*, which involved treason against the emperor and the State, the two being regarded as one entity. At this stage in Nero's reign the cult of emperor was such that he was virtually deified, and he also wielded plenary power in civil, military, legal and religious affairs. It is easy to see that in this atmosphere a charge that Paul was promoting a rival King, and a religion not authorised by the State, could be used to secure his downfall, even if due legal process were followed.

In practice the emperor's authority was such that due legal process could be manipulated to accommodate his personal views.

Paul's trial

The emperor had unlimited legal competence and could function as a court of last instance, so that there was no further recourse for an appellant whose case had been refused. He did not, however, hear every case himself, tending to reserve his attention for those involving persons of high rank, or grave questions of State security, and delegating others to officials. Nero is said to have heard far fewer cases than his predecessor, Claudius. Paul's appeal, however, had been to Caesar himself, and the angel who stood by Paul during the shipwreck had assured him that *thou must stand before Caesar* (Acts 27: 24).

The character of Paul's trial was probably a *cognitio* which was a full judicial trial involving the admission of evidence, and handing down a judgement. Procedure was initiated by accusers who submitted written or oral charges, and the accused was allowed to make a personal defence, an *apologia*. In cases heard by the emperor or his delegates this defence was often made without an *advocatus*.

No one stood with Paul at his first trial. No *advocatus* to defend him. No *patronus* to support him. No witnesses. No sympathisers. It is easy to understand that the viciousness of a demented emperor, and the refined cruelty of Tigellinus, his depraved lieutenant, would strike fear into the hearts of the Roman Christians. Paul does not blame them: but what a sad situation that there was not a single person to be found when the great apostle most needed support! Nevertheless the Lord stood with him. Nero did not see Him standing there, but the apostle was conscious of His presence and his bold testimony rang out in power in the crowded court.

If Paul's case was heard by the emperor himself, what a contrast between the two men! In the place of authority a man vile and degraded, not shrinking from the murder of his own mother, living a debauched and profligate life. And facing him, although a prisoner, the greatest man after Christ who had ever lived upon the earth, one who had exhausted all his strength in the most extraordinary service to humanity. Just as good and evil met at the cross of Christ, so these forces confronted one another in a Roman court.

Roman trials
In a Roman trial each voter was given three tablets, one marked A for *absolve*; another with C for *condemno*; and a third with N.L. for *non liquet*, not proven. The result of Paul's first hearing was evidently *non liquet* resulting in an *ampliatio*, or postponement. It seems, however, from his second letter to Timothy that he realised this was only a delay and the end was inevitable.

Obverse of a gold aureus coin (valued at 25 silver denarii) with the image of the Emperor Nero wearing a laurel wreath, inscribed NERO CAESAR AVGVSTVS.

After this preliminary hearing the emperor could consult his advisers before giving judgement. The fact that Paul was *delivered out of the lion's mouth* (2 Timothy 4: 17) suggests that the power of his defence effectively refuted the evil charges against him, at least for a time, although still leaving him a prisoner.

Use diligence to come before winter.

2 Timothy 4: 21

It is at this point that the great apostle wrote his second letter to Timothy, urging him to come to him before winter. Ephesus was about 1,100 miles (1,770 km) distant so it would have taken a messenger up to two months to reach Timothy, and another two months for Timothy to reach Rome. This would be especially so if Timothy had to go by Troas to collect Paul's cloak, books and parchments, and then travel overland from Neapolis along the *Via Egnatia*, rather than take the quicker sea route from Ephesus. Whether he arrived in Rome before Paul died we do not know. Nor do we know what happened at a subsequent hearing, and how the apostle was condemned.

The greatest martyr

Paul never forgave himself for persecuting the church and knew, from the first time Christ spoke to him, that he would die a martyr's death. He looked forward to this as an honour. Far from being afraid, it was a joy to him, and Nero's sword was not of the least consequence to the apostle. But he also accepted it as governmentally right that he should suffer imprisonment and death because of what he had done to Christ's saints. Paul welcomed death. The Lord could have kept him alive, but Paul made the decision to go to be with Christ, and the judgement of the court was merely an instrument.

No account exists of the apostle's last moments but according to tradition he was led outside the city walls, and executed by the Roman sword, the prescribed method for a Roman citizen condemned to death. The details are obscure, but what we can be certain of is that the Lord's beloved and honoured servant, when the time of his release came, had fulfilled his commission and perfectly completed the work given to him.

SECTION 5

APPENDICES

PAUL'S COMPANIONS

A

Persons who came into contact with Paul during his journeys, and were favourable to him, include the following:

ACHAICUS   a brother from Corinth whose visit to Paul at Ephesus, with Stephanus and Fortunatus, gave the apostle joy and refreshment (1 Corinthians 16: 17, 18).

AGABUS   a prophet from Jerusalem who foresaw a great famine (Acts 11: 28) and in Philip's house at Caesarea predicted Paul's arrest at Jerusalem (Acts 21: 10, 11).

ANANIAS   a disciple at Damascus, the first to greet Saul after his conversion (Acts 9: 10–17). In his address to the Jews at Jerusalem (Acts 22: 12) Paul emphasised the Jewish credentials of Ananias.

APOLLOS   an Alexandrian Jew, converted to Christianity, who came to Ephesus where he was instructed by Aquila and Priscilla, and then served in Achaia after being given a letter of commendation from Ephesus (Acts 18: 24–28). Paul warned the Corinthians against making Apollos the leader of a faction (1 Corinthians 1: 12; 3: 4–6, 22). Later, sensitive as to this danger, Apollos was unwilling to return to Corinth (1 Corinthians 16: 12). Paul subsequently gave instructions to Titus regarding Apollos and Zenas (Titus 3: 13).

APPHIA   a sister, presumed to be Philemon's wife, and included in the opening salutations of Paul's letter to him (Philemon 2).

AQUILA AND PRISCILLA (PRISCA)   husband and wife who first met Paul at Corinth, on his second journey: he lodged and worked with them since, like him, they were tent makers (Acts 18: 1, 2). They had moved to Corinth from Italy after the emperor, Claudius, had ordered all Jews to leave Rome. They then moved with Paul to Ephesus, where they helped Apollos, and were with Paul when he wrote his first letter to the Corinthians (1 Corinthians 16: 19). After the death of Claudius they returned to Rome and are included in Paul's salutation to the brethren there (Romans 16: 3) with the commendation that they *for my life staked their own neck*: it may be they rescued Paul at the time of the riot in Ephesus. Aquila was a Jew, from Pontus. Priscilla may have been a Gentile, possibly connected with the *gens prisca*, one of the leading families in Rome: if so, her higher social standing would explain why she is sometimes put first, before Aquila. Paul again saluted them in his second letter to Timothy (4: 19).

ARCHIPPUS a brother at Colosse whom Paul describes as a fellow soldier (Philemon 2) and whom he exhorts to fulfil the ministry he had received from the Lord (Colossians 4: 17).

ARISTARCHUS a Macedonian of Thessalonica and fellow traveller of Paul who was seized in the riot at Ephesus. He travelled with the apostle as far as Asia (Acts 20: 4) and was with Paul on the voyage from Caesarea to Rome, appearing in the salutations in the epistles to the Colossians (4: 10) and Philemon (24), written from Rome.

ARTEMAS apparently a fellow worker whom Paul intended to send to Crete to relieve Titus (Titus 3: 12).

BARNABAS (JOSEPH SURNAMED BARNABAS) a levite, Cyprian by birth (Acts 4: 36, 37) who introduced Saul to the apostles (Acts 9: 27) and later brought him from Tarsus to help with the work at Antioch (Acts 11: 25, 26). Some have wondered if he had previous acquaintance with Paul, possibly through studying at Tarsus. He accompanied Paul on his first missionary journey (Acts 13, 14), and to the conference at Jerusalem (Acts 15) but separated from him after a disagreement over Mark (Acts 15: 36–40) who was evidently his cousin (Colossians 4: 10). In the early days of the church Barnabas sold land and made the proceeds available to the apostles (Acts 4: 37).

CARPUS evidently a householder at Troas, where Paul had left his cloak (2 Timothy 4: 13).

CHLOE a sister, apparently from Corinth (1 Corinthians 1: 11). Members of her house had reported to Paul about conditions at Corinth, possibly when he was in Ephesus.

CLAUDIA presumably a sister at Rome, who sent greetings to Timothy (2 Timothy 4: 21). Some have identified her as the wife of Pudens, based on a mention in the epigrams of Martial, a first century poet.

CLEMENT a fellow labourer of Paul mentioned in Philippians (4: 3), thought by some to be Clement of Rome, an early church father (see page 116).

CRESCENS a disciple who had evidently been with Paul at Rome, but had gone to Galatia (2 Timothy 4: 10).

CRISPUS the ruler of the synagogue at Corinth who was converted to Christianity, with all his house (Acts 18: 8). He was baptised by Paul (1 Corinthians 1: 14).

DAMARIS a woman who believed after hearing Paul's address to the Areopagites (Acts 17: 34).

DEMAS a Colossian who visited Paul in Rome: the apostle included him with other fellow workmen in Philemon 24 and mentioned him to the Colossians (4: 14). However he forsook Paul at the end of the apostle's life, loving the present age (2 Timothy 4: 10).

DIONYSIUS a member of the Areopagus, the former supreme court in Athens, who believed after hearing Paul's address (Acts 17: 34). Areopagites had to be over 60 years old, and to have filled a high magisterial function.

EPAENETUS a believer at Rome, evidently one of the first to be converted in Asia, to whom Paul sent greetings (Romans 16: 5).

EPAPHRAS a brother from Colosse who visited Paul in Rome and combated in prayer for the Colossians (Colossians 1: 7, 4: 12; Philemon 23).

EPAPHRODITUS a brother from Philippi who brought supplies to Paul when the apostle was a prisoner in Rome and who was sick *close to death*. Paul wrote warmly of his service (Philippians 2: 25–30, 4: 18).

ERASTUS one who ministered to Paul at Ephesus, and was sent to Macedonia with Timotheus (Acts 19: 22). This may be the same Erastus as in Romans 16: 23 where he is referred to as the steward of the city (Corinth). In 2 Timothy 4: 20 Paul refers to Erastus remaining in Corinth.

EUBULUS presumably a local brother at Rome, who sent greetings to Timothy (2 Timothy 4: 21).

EUTYCHUS a youth who fell from the third story during Paul's long discourse at Troas (Acts 20: 9–12) and was restored to life by the apostle.

FORTUNATUS a brother from Corinth whose visit to Paul at Ephesus, with Stephanus and Achaicus, gave the apostle joy and refreshment (1 Corinthians 16: 17, 18).

GAIUS (OF MACEDONIA) a fellow traveller of Paul who was seized by the mob in the riot at Ephesus (Acts 19: 29). This is probably the same Gaius as Acts 20: 4.

GAIUS (OF CORINTH) a believer baptised by Paul (1 Corinthians 1: 14) who was evidently his host at Corinth when he wrote the epistle to the Romans (Romans 16: 23).

THE JAILOR AT PHILIPPI was convicted and found salvation after Paul saved him from taking his life, following the earthquake. After washing Paul and Silas from the bloody weals resulting from their being beaten he and his household were baptised, and showed Paul and Silas hospitality (Acts 16: 27–34).

JAMES brother of the Lord (Matthew 13: 55) and writer of the epistle of James became the leading figure in the Jerusalem assembly. Paul met him on his first visit to Jerusalem after his conversion (Galatians 1: 19). On his second visit 14 years later James, Cephas and John accepted that Paul had his own commission to evangelise the Gentiles (Galatians 2: 7–10). James made the decisive speech in the Acts 15 conference, confirming that believing Gentiles should not be made subject to Jewish law. On Paul's final visit to Jerusalem James, unable to restrain the strong Judaising element, suggested the vow which indirectly led to Paul's arrest (Acts 21: 20–24). Known as 'James the Just' on account of his piety he was ultimately challenged by the orthodox Jews about his faith in Jesus, thrown down from a pinnacle of the temple and murdered, in 62 AD.

JASON the host of Paul and Silas at Thessalonica, who was dragged before the magistrates and forced to provide security for his guests (Acts 17: 5–9). A Jason is included, with two others, in those sending salutations in Paul's letter to the Romans (16: 21), which was written subsequently from Corinth: they are designated as *my kinsmen*.

JESUS CALLED JUSTUS a fellow worker with Paul, one of the few Jewish ones who had been a consolation to him (Colossians 4: 10, 11).

JOHN the apostle: there is only one record of a meeting between John and Paul, in Galatians 2: 9.

JUDAS CALLED BARSABAS one of the delegates who accompanied Paul and Barnabas back to Antioch, to convey the findings of the conference at Jerusalem (Acts 15: 22).

JULIUS a centurion of Augustus' company who was responsible for transporting Paul from Caesarea to Rome (Acts 27: 1). By the end of the voyage he had begun to appreciate the distinctiveness of the apostle, and refused to allow him, and the other prisoners, to be killed when they were landing at Malta (Acts 27: 43).

JUSTUS Paul's host at Corinth (Acts 18: 7) after he experienced opposition from the Jews. Justus was a Gentile worshipper who attended the synagogue adjoining his house. He may have been one of the original members of the Roman colony introduced into Corinth.

LINUS presumably a brother at Rome, who sent greetings to Timothy (2 Timothy 4: 21).

LUCIUS a kinsman of Paul who sent his salutations to the Romans (Romans 16: 21).

LUKE writer of Luke's Gospel and the Acts. He was with Paul in three sections of the Acts, according to his use of the pronoun 'we' rather than 'they': chapters 16: 10 to 17: 1; 20: 5 to 21: 18; and 27: 1 to the end of the book. He was with Paul in Rome (Colossians 4: 14, Philemon 24), and remained with him near the end of the apostle's life (2 Timothy 4: 11). It is assumed he was a Gentile since he is not included in Colossians 4: 10, 11 with those described as *of the circumcision*. Luke was a physician (Colossians 4: 14): it has been speculated that he may have studied at the most celebrated medical school of the day, which was at Tarsus, and could have had previous contact with Paul. According to Eusebius (Ecclesiastical History iii.4) he was a doctor from Antioch in Syria, and this is confirmed by Jerome.

LYDIA a Gentile woman who attended Jewish worship, whose heart was opened after hearing the words of Paul at Philippi (Acts 16: 13–15). She offered the apostle hospitality, and Paul and Silas went to her house after being released from prison (Acts 16: 40). She originated from Thyatira and sold the purple dyes for which that region was famous.

MARK (JOHN, surnamed MARK) son of Mary, of Jerusalem (Acts 12: 12) and relative of Barnabas, described as his *cousin* in Colossians 4: 10 (AV *sister's son to Barnabas*). He accompanied Paul and Barnabas as an attendant on the first missionary journey (Acts 13: 5) but abandoned them at Perga of Pamphylia (Acts 13: 13). Paul refused Barnabas's suggestion to take Mark with them on the second journey (Acts 15: 38). He was, however, with Paul at Rome (Colossians 4: 10, Philemon 24). At the end of his life Paul asked Timothy to bring Mark with him (2 Timothy 4: 11). He is believed to be author of the Gospel according to Mark.

MNASON a Cyprian, who accompanied Paul from Caesarea to Jerusalem, and gave him lodgings the night before he met with James and the elders, on his last visit. Presumably it would have been too sensitive for a mixed company of Jews and Gentiles to be accommodated in a Jewish household at Jerusalem:

Mnason, a Hellenist, had no such scruples. He is described as an old disciple, meaning he had been involved in the testimony from the beginning: he may have been one of the Cyprians who preached at Antioch (Acts 11: 20).

NYMPHAS a brother, apparently from Laodicea, who had the assembly in his house and was saluted by Paul (Colossians 4: 17).

ONESIMUS a slave of Philemon, apparently from Colosse, who had run away from his master and encountered Paul, when a prisoner in Rome. Under the apostle's influence he repented and became submissive: Paul wrote to Philemon and the assembly in his house commending Onesimus, who returned with the letter in the company of Tychicus. Paul referred to him again, apparently, in Colossians 4: 9.

ONESIPHORUS a disciple who had rendered service in Ephesus and who searched diligently for Paul when he was a prisoner in Rome, and found him (2 Timothy 1: 16–18, 4: 19). The apostle appreciated his loyalty at a time when many were turning away, and some were ashamed to associate with a prisoner.

PAUL'S SISTER'S SON a youth who informed Paul of a Jewish plot to kill him and who, on the apostle's instructions, told his story to the chiliarch, Claudius Lysias (Acts 23: 16–22).

PETER (CEPHAS) one of the twelve and the apostle of the circumcision whose powerful preaching resulted in three thousand souls being added (Acts 2: 41). Paul went to Jerusalem to make acquaintance with him (Galatians 1: 18) and again met him at the Acts 15 conference (Galatians 2: 9). When Peter visited Antioch he was withstood by Paul because he had gone back, under strong pressure, on the question of eating with Gentile believers (Galatians 2: 11). In his second epistle he acknowledged Paul's wisdom and put his writings on the level of Scripture (2 Peter 3: 15, 16).

PHOEBE served as a deaconess in the assembly in Cenchrea, the eastern sea port for Corinth: Paul commended her to the Romans saying she had helped many, including himself (Romans 16: 1). She may have taken the epistle, which was written at Corinth, to Rome.

PHILEMON a brother, possibly from Colosse, who had the assembly in his house, and whose slave, Onesimus, met Paul at Rome and was converted by him. In Paul's epistle to Philemon, written from Rome, he asked him to prepare him a lodging (verse 22), indicating he expected to be released.

PHILIP the evangelist, one of the seven men appointed to oversee the daily ministration (Acts 6: 5), and whose preaching converted the Ethiopian eunuch (Acts 8: 35). Paul stayed in his house at Caesarea on his last visit to Jerusalem (Acts 21: 8). He had four virgin daughters who prophesied.

PRISCILLA (PRISCA) – see **AQUILA AND PRISCILLA (PRISCA)**

PUBLIUS an official in Malta designated *chief man of the island* which was an official title, *Protos Melitaion*. He gave Paul and Luke, and possibly others, hospitality for three days. Paul cured his father from fever and dysentery (Acts 28: 7, 8).

PUDENS presumably a brother local at Rome, who sent greetings to Timothy (2 Timothy 4: 21). See **CLAUDIA**.

QUARTUS a brother who sent his salutations to the Romans (Romans 16: 23).

ROMAN BRETHREN Paul named twenty-six persons in his salutations to the brethren at Rome (Romans 16: 3–15). No doubt he had met many of these and knew them even although he had not yet visited Rome at the time the epistle was written.

SECUNDUS a Thessalonian who accompanied Paul from Greece as far as Asia (Acts 20:4), possibly assisting with transportation of the collection for Jerusalem.

SILAS (SILVANUS) one of the delegates who accompanied Paul and Barnabas back to Antioch, to convey the findings of the conference at Jerusalem (Acts 15: 22). He was attracted to what he found at Antioch and remained there when Judas called Barsabas returned to Jerusalem (Acts 15: 34, AV). He accompanied Paul on his second missionary journey, was imprisoned with him at Philippi (Acts 16: 19–25), joined him at Corinth (Acts 18: 5) and preached there (2 Corinthians 1: 19). Acts 16: 37 may indicate he was a Roman citizen. He is presumed to be the amanuensis of Peter's first epistle (1 Peter 5: 12).

SOPATER SON OF PYRRHUS a Berean who accompanied Paul from Greece as far as Asia (Acts 20: 4), possibly assisting with transportation of the collection for Jerusalem.

SOSIPATER a kinsman of Paul who sent his salutations to the Romans (Romans 16: 21).

SOSTHENES the ruler of the synagogue at Corinth who was beaten before Gallio's judgement seat, possibly by the anti Jewish crowd (Acts 18: 17). The Sosthenes included in Paul's salutation to the Corinthians (1 Corinthians 1: 1) may be the same person, since the name was relatively rare: if so, he had clearly become converted to Christianity.

STEPHANAS a brother at Corinth whose household was baptised by Paul (1 Corinthians 1: 16). Paul refers to his house as the *first-fruits of Achaia* and writes of the joy and refreshment he experienced when Stephanus, Fortunatus and Achaicus came to Paul at Ephesus. (1 Corinthians 16: 15–18).

TERTIUS Paul's amanuensis for his letter to the Romans, who added his own greeting (Romans 16: 22).

TIMOTHY (TIMOTHEUS) faithful follower of Paul who may have heard the apostle on his first visit to Lycaonia, but was selected for service on his second visit (Acts 16: 1–3). He was of mixed parentage and Paul circumcised him to pre-empt Jewish opposition. He accompanied Paul on his second and third journeys and was with him at Rome. At some stage Timothy was imprisoned himself (Hebrews 13: 23). Paul addressed two letters to him, the second from Rome, towards the end of his life, urging Timothy to come to him quickly.

TITUS a gentile, uncircumcised, whom Paul took with him to Jerusalem for the Acts 15 conference (Galatians 2: 3). On Paul's third journey Titus met him in Macedonia with a cheering report from Corinth regarding the reception of Paul's first letter (2 Corinthians 7: 5–7). Paul described him as his *companion and fellow labourer* (2 Corinthians 8: 23) and who walked in the same spirit and steps as the apostle (2 Corinthians 12: 18). Paul left Titus in Crete with detailed instructions how to address conditions there (Titus 1–3), but with directions to come to him at Nicopolis as soon as Artemas or Tychicus arrive (Titus 3: 12).

TROPHIMUS a believer from Ephesus who travelled with Paul from Greece to Asia (Acts 20:4), possibly assisting with transportation of the collection for Jerusalem, and went on to Jerusalem. Jews from Asia who saw Trophimus with Paul in the city there wrongly assumed the apostle had taken him into the area of the temple forbidden to Gentiles, and started the riot which led to Paul's arrest (Acts 21: 27–30). In his second letter Paul tells Timothy he had left Trophimus behind at Miletus, sick (2 Timothy 4: 20).

TYCHICUS a believer from Asia who accompanied Paul from Greece as far as Asia (Acts 20: 4), possibly assisting with transportation of the collection for Jerusalem. He visited Paul during his imprisonment at Rome and was entrusted with delivery of the apostle's letters to the brethren at Ephesus and Colosse (Ephesians 6: 21, Colossians 4: 7), as well as his letter to Philemon. He returned to Asia with Onesimus. Later Paul told Timothy he had sent him to Ephesus (2 Timothy 4: 12), and told Titus that he may send him to Crete (Titus 3: 12).

ZENAS a lawyer who had evidently visited Titus in Crete (Titus 3: 13). Paul directed Titus to ensure he and Apollos lacked nothing on their onward journey.

CHRONOLOGY

It is possible to work out the length of Paul's service, from his conversion to the end of the Acts, at around 29 years, as follows:

Conversion to first Jerusalem visit (Galatians 1: 18)	3 years
Period to third Jerusalem visit (Acts 15, Galatians 2: 1)	14 years
Second western journey	3 years
Third western journey	5 years
From Paul's arrest, to the end of the Acts	4 years

We do not, however, know any dates – not even of Paul's birth, his conversion, his service nor his death. Any dates given are calculated, and involve assumptions.

The problem is that although we know the dates of many historical events in the first century, from the writings of Tacitus (56–117 AD), Josephus (37–c100 AD) and others, there are no points of synchronism where these historical events can be related with certainty to Christian events.

Scholars have studied this question for many years, and the fact there is little consensus shows how intractable the problem is. However an approximate timeline can be worked out which gets us within a few years of events in the Acts, based on the following reasoning:

Paul's escape from Damascus The escape described in Acts 9: 25 and 2 Corinthians 11: 32, 33 was apparently after Paul's return to the city from Arabia, and evidently took place during the reign of Aretas IV Philopatris, who ruled the Nabataean kingdom from c 9 BC, and died in 40 AD. Initially this seems a promising line of enquiry to establish the date of Paul's escape, and therefore of his conversion, three years or more previously. However scholars are not agreed when Aretas IV took control of Damascus: some say the city came under Nabataean rule from around 85 BC, and that King Aretas III became a Roman vassal after Pompey invaded Palestine in 63 BC; others think it more likely that Aretas IV did not rule Damascus until 37 AD after Tiberius died, in a settlement with Caligula. If we take 40 AD as the latest possible date for Paul's escape (being the year of the death of King Aretas IV), and of his first visit to Jerusalem (Galatians 1: 18), and add fourteen years (Galatians 2:1), this takes us to around 54 AD for the date of the Acts 15 visit, assuming that is the same visit as referred to in Galatians 2: 1–10, and remembering that the 14 years may include part years. Of course the visit to Jerusalem may have been earlier, and many scholars have settled on 37 AD, which would make the Acts 15 visit nearer 51 AD. If we take 60 AD as the date of Paul's departure for Rome and work backwards it has been calculated the second western journey must have started in 51, which confirms the date of the Acts 15 visit as around that time.

Death of Agrippa I Agrippa died in Caesarea (Acts 12: 23) in the third year of his reign, which had begun in 41 AD, so this gives us a date of 44 AD. Orosius (c375 to c418) also gives 44 as the year of the famine which devastated Judea, but Josephus makes it later, at 46 AD, the famine no doubt lasting several years. The famine is given in Luke's account (Acts 11: 27–30, 12: 25) as the reason for Paul's second visit to Jerusalem after his conversion.

The appointment of Gallio as proconsul Scholars have attempted to establish the date of Paul's hearing before Gallio (Acts 18: 12–17) by reference to the Delphi inscription, a copy of a letter from the emperor, Claudius, to the citizens of Delphi, in which he refers to "my friend Gallio, proconsul of Achaia". This is dated in the period of Claudius's twenty-sixth acclamation as imperator, which equates to the first seven months of 52.

Paul's visit to Troas in Acts 20 Recent research has concluded that the date of Paul's visit to Troas in Acts 20 was 58 AD. This has been arrived at, firstly, by establishing the period of time between the feast of the Passover and the first day of the week at Troas (Acts 20: 7) as 17 days, based on the detail given in Acts 20: 6, 7. Since there is a correlation between the timing of the Passover feast and the moon phase (see Exodus 12: 2 and 6), with the full moon falling on the fifteenth day of the Jewish month, the next step was to identify the year in which the seventeenth day after the full moon fell on a Sunday (the first day of the week in Acts 20: 7), which was done by researching reliable astronomical data. The only year between 56 and 60 AD, inclusive, which fulfils the criteria is 58 AD, and the day of the apostle's long discourse is identified as Sunday, 29th May (Julian day 1742376). If this conclusion becomes authenticated it represents a significant breakthrough in our understanding of the chronology of the apostle's life.

Paul's voyage to Rome Eusebius (263–339) gives 55 AD as the date of the recall of Felix to Rome (Acts 24: 27) although most scholars consider it was later, probably 60. Pallas, the brother of Felix, who saved him from punishment, was executed by Nero in 62, but could still have been influential two years earlier. Paul's case was heard by Festus soon after he became Procurator and he was sent to Rome under the care of Julius in Autumn of the same year, arriving in Rome the following Spring, after wintering in Malta. If the year that Paul sailed from Caesarea was indeed 60, so that he arrived in Rome in the Spring of 61, after wintering in Malta, two years' house imprisonment in Rome takes us to 63, when Paul may possibly have been released. There is uncertainty about the final stages of his life, except that persecution of Christians followed the Great Fire of Rome in 64, and by then the persons in the government favourable to the apostle had died. However there is no certainty about the dates of Paul's final trials, nor of his death.

Governors of Judea

Rule by Rome over Judea, and later over most of Palestine, came into force in the year 6 AD after Herod's son, Archelaus, was banished, and continued to 66, with an interruption of three years, 41 to 44, during the reign of Agrippa I. The governors took the title of Procurator (or Prefect) and held the power of capital punishment (*jus gladii*). However Roman citizens had the right to have their cases heard by the emperor instead of the provincial governor, and the Procurator was subject to the Roman legate in Syria. The Procurator resided at Caesarea, where he had his *praetorium*, the former palace of Herod, and visited Jerusalem only on special occasions. His *praetorium* there was in the fortress of Antonia, again a former palace of Herod.

	AD
Coponus	6–9
Marcus Ambibulus	9–12
Rufus Tineus	12–15
Valerius Gratus	15–26
Pontius Pilate	26–36
Marcellus	37–41
Herod Agrippa I	41–44
Cuspius Fadus	44–46
Tiberius Julius Alexander	46–48
Ventidius Cumanus	48–52
Marcus Antonius Felix	52–60
Porcius Festus	60–62
Lucius Albinus	62–64
Gessius Florus	64–66

Timeline of events

There is uncertainty about the precise timing of Assembly Events and the dates given below should be regarded as approximate.

YEAR AD	ASSEMBLY EVENTS	CONTEMPORARY EVENTS
34	Martyrdom of Stephen	
34	Paul's conversion	
34–37	Paul in Arabia	
37	Paul escapes from Damascus, Acts 9: 25	
37	Paul's first visit to Jerusalem after his conversion	
41		Herod Agrippa I made King of Judea by Claudius
43		Claudius conquers Britain
44	Execution of James, brother of John, Acts 12: 1–2	Death of Herod Agrippa I, Acts 12
45	Paul's second visit to Jerusalem, with Barnabas, Acts 11: 30	
46–48		
48–49		Agrippa II (Acts 25) made King of Chalcis
49		Seneca appointed as Nero's tutor
50		Caractacus captured by the Romans in Britain
50		Claudius expels the Jews from Rome, Acts 18: 2
51	Paul's third visit to Jerusalem, Acts 15, Galatians 2: 1–10	Afranius Burrus appointed Prefect of Praetorian Guards
51–52		Gallio proconsul of Achaia
51–53	Paul's second western journey	
52		
53		Tetrarchy of Trachonitis given to Agrippa II
53–58	Paul's third western journey	
54		
58	Paul's arrest at Jerusalem, Acts 21: 33	
58–60	Paul held as a prisoner at Caesarea	
59		Nero's mother, Agrippina the Younger, put to death
60	(Autumn) start of voyage to Rome – shipwreck at Malta, Acts 27	Felix recalled to Rome and succeeded by Festus
61	Paul's arrival at Rome	Revolt in Britain under Boadicea, Queen of the Iceni
61–63	Paul in his own hired lodging at Rome, Acts 28: 30–31	
62		Burrus dies, Tigellinus made Praetorian Prefect
62		Nero marries Poppaea
64	Paul's martyrdom	Great fire of Rome, followed by persecution of Christians
65		Seneca commits suicide; death of Poppaea
66–70		First Jewish war against the Romans
68		

Paul's age

If we make assumptions (a) that Paul's conversion was in 34 AD; (b) that he was 27 at that time; and (c) that he was martyred in 64 AD, we can surmise that he was born in 7 AD and was 57 years old when he died.

EMPERORS	RULERS OF JUDEA	YEAR AD
		34
		34
Tiberius 14–37	Pontius Pilate 26–36, Marcellus 36–37	34–37
Caligula 37–41	Marullus 37–41	37
		37
Claudius 41–54	King Herod Agrippa I 41–44	41
		43
	Cuspius Fadus 44–46	44
		45
	Tiberius Alexander 46–48	46–48
	Ventidius Cumanus 48–52	48–49
		49
		50
		50
		51
		51–52
		51–53
	Antonius Felix 52–60	52
		53
		53–58
Nero 54–68		54
		58
		59–60
		59
	Porcius Festus 60–62	60
		61
		61–63
	Lucius Albinus 62–64	62
		62
	Gessius Florus 64–66	64
		65
		66–70
Death of Nero		68

GLOSSARY

ABSOLVE	to pronounce not guilty, in a Roman court
ACTI PAULI	an apocryphal work about Paul
ACROPOLIS	the citadel of Athens, site of the Parthenon temple
ADVOCATUS	a legal advocate
AGORA	centre of civic life in Athens and other Greek cities
AMPLIATIO	adjournment or postponement of a Roman court case
APOLOGIA	a defence of one's belief or conduct
APOCRYPHAL	counterfeit, or of questionable authenticity
ARAMAIC	a Semitic language spoken by the Jews in Palestine
AREOPAGUS	a hill to the northwest of the Acropolis in Athens, and the name of the judicial council that met there
AV	Authorised (King James) Version of the Bible
BARBARIAN	a term applied to all nations not of Greek or Roman descent, and speaking a foreign language
'CAESAREM APELLO'	*I appeal to Caesar* – the right of a Roman citizen to appeal to the emperor
CATACUMBAS	catacombs, subterranean tunnels in Rome used as burial places
CAVEAT	a warning or caution
CHILIARCH	a Roman officer in charge of a thousand men
CILICIUM	a textile, woven in Cilicia from goats' hair, used for tent making
'CIVIS ROMANUS SUM'	*I am a Roman citizen* – words spoken to assert the right of a Roman citizen to be exempted from degrading punishment
CIVITAS	Roman citizenship
CIVITATES LIBERAE	Roman cities which were virtually self governing
CIVITATES STIPENDARIAE	tributary Roman cities
COGNITIO	a full Roman judicial trial
COGNOMEN	a name given to distinguish a branch of a family
COHORT	a unit of six *centuria*, each of 80 to 100 men and commanded by a centurion, with the most senior centurion commanding the cohort
COLONIAE	Roman colonies
CONDEMNO	a sentence of guilty in a Roman court
CRIMEN LAESAE MAIESTATIS	an offence committed against the sovereign power in a state; treason (see **MAIESTATIS**)
CURSUS PUBLICUS	the state run courier and transportation system of the Roman Empire, the most highly developed postal system of the ancient world
CUSTODIA LIBERA	a form of probation by which a prisoner was allowed freedom, but his friends were made responsible for his safekeeping and appearance at a trial
CUSTODIA MILITARIS	a form of Roman custody in which the prisoner could choose his own place of residence, but was accompanied by a soldier, and chained to him if he left the house

CUSTODIA PUBLICA	penal detention in which the prisoner was chained and imprisoned
DIALECTIC	disputation or debate
DIALKOS	a roadway made to allow small ships to be portaged across the isthmus between the western and eastern harbours at Corinth
DIOSCURI	in Greek mythology the Dioscuri were Castor and Polydeuces (or Pollux), twin sons of Leda and Zeus and the brothers of Helen of Troy
DULCIS GALLIO	a familiar name given to Gallio, proconsul of Corinth
DUUMVIRI	Roman city magistrates
DIPLOMATA	an official pass carried by Roman soldiers and officials empowering them to compel civilians to provide assistance (Matthew 5: 41)
EDOMITE	a descendant of Esau, eldest son of Isaac and Rebecca
EPICUREAN	a school of philosophy following the teachings of Epicurus, 341–270 BC
EUROCLYDON	a violent, cyclonic wind which blows in the Mediterranean
EXEGESIS	critical interpretation of a text, especially Scripture
FASCES	a bundle of rods 1.5 metres (5 feet) long and a single headed axe bound together by red tape and carried by Lictors as an expression of magisterial authority (see Acts 16: 23)
FIRST TRIUMVIRATE	a political alliance of Julius Caesar, Licinius Crassus and Pompeius Magnus towards the end of the Roman Republic around 60 BC
FORUM	open space in the centre of Rome, or other Roman cities, the centre of Roman public life
FOSSA	a trench or ditch at the side of a Roman road
FRUMENTARII	officials who supervised transportation of grain to Rome
GAZITH	hall of meeting for the Sanhedrim in Jerusalem
GENS PRISCA	one of the leading families in Rome
GENTILICIUM	a family name, also called **NOMEN**
HASMONEANS	the ruling dynasty which achieved Jewish independence in Israel for about 80 years following the collapse of the Seleucid kingdom in 129 BC
HELLENISM	Greek culture and influence which prevailed in the ancient world following the conquests of Alexander the Great, and his death in 323 BC
HELLENIST	a non-Greek, especially a Jew, who adopted Greek culture and language
IDES OF MARCH	15th March in the Roman calendar
IMPERATOR	a title of the emperor
IUS SEPULCRI	the right of a Roman citizen to burial
JUDAISERS	a designation for Jewish Christians who insisted Gentile believers observed Jewish law and practices
KALENDS (or CALENDS)	the first day of each month in the ancient Roman calendar
KOINE	the ancient Greek dialect that became the lingua franca of the Hellenist world and considered by some to be the Greek of the New Testament
LEVANT	a name for the eastern Mediterranean area, now occupied by Lebanon, Syria and Israel
LEX PORCIA	Roman laws enacted between 199 and 184 BC giving the right of appeal (provocatio) against scourging, and in capital cases
LICTORS	Roman officials who attended the Praetors and administered punishment by means of fasces
LINGUA FRANCA	a language used for communication between people of different mother tongues
LIBERA CUSTODIA	a form of probation by which a prisoner was allowed freedom, but his friends were made responsible for his safekeeping and appearance at a trial

LOCUS RELIGIOSUS	a grave or tomb protected by the state from desecration
MACCABEES	descendants of Mattathias the Hasmonean, who ruled Judea after the Maccabean revolt (see **HASMONEANS**)
MAIESTAS	short for *minuta populi romani*, the dimunition of the majesty of the Roman people, a crime introduced in the *lex Appuleia* c103 BC, used against treason or conspiracy
MANSIONS	stopping places on Roman roads, especially for the *cursus publicus*
MANUMISSION	emancipation from the state of slavery
MARE CLAUSUM	closure of the seas for sailing between 10th November and 10th March
MARE NOSTRUM	'our sea' – Roman name for the Mediterranean
MEMORIAE	monuments or shrines erected at the burial places of martyrs
MILIARIUS AUREM	a golden zero milestone erected by Augustus in the Forum of ancient Rome from which all Roman roads began, and from which distances were measured
NAZARITE	a Jew who made a vow of dedication to Jehovah, for a specific period or for life (see Numbers 6: 1–21)
NAVES CAUDICARIAE	small ships used to transport cargo between the port of Ostia and Rome
NAVIGIUM ISIDIS	a festival held in March to celebrate the opening of the seas
NOMEN	a family name, also called **GENTILICIUM**
NON LIQET	a verdict of *not proven* in a Roman court
OPPIDIUM DEVIUM	Cicero's description of Berea: *an out-of-the-way town*
ORARIIS NAVIBUS	coasting vessels
PANTHEISM	a doctrine that regards God as identical with the material and natural universe
PARTHENON	the temple on the Acropolis at Athens
PATRISTIC	leaders ('Fathers') of the early church especially in the first five centuries AD
PATRONUS	in Roman society, a protector, sponsor or benefactor of a client, including legal representation (see 1 John 2: 1)
PAX ROMANA	a period of relative peace, law and order, economic prosperity and cultural achievement between the accession of Augustus in 27 BC and the death of Marcus Aurelius in 180 AD. There can be no doubt the *Pax Romana* facilitated the spread of Paul's glad tidings
PHARISEES	a Jewish party noted for exact observance of the law and claiming superior sanctity
POLIS	a Greek city, or citizenship; city-state
POLITARCHS	the title for the city magistrates of Thessalonica
POPULOUS ROMANUS	the right of appeal to the Roman people; a collective term for the Roman citizen body (see **PROVOCATIO**)
PRAENOMEN	the personal name given to a Roman male, such as *Tertius*, the third
PRAETORS	another name for Roman magistrates
PRAETORIUM	the headquarters of the Imperial Guard, whether at Caesarea (Acts 23: 35) or Rome (Philippians 1: 13)
PROCURATOR	a Roman official, often governor of a minor province (from the Latin verb *procurare* 'to take care of, manage')
PROCONSUL	the governor of a senatorial province in ancient Rome
PROSELYTE	one newly converted to a religious faith
PROVINCIAE	Roman provinces, the largest administrative and territorial units in the empire
PROVOCATIO	the right to appeal against the ruling of a magistrate to the *comitia populi tribute* (assembly of citizens), secured by the *Lex Valeria* of 300 BC. The cry *provoco ad populum* compelled a magistrate to wait for the intervention and ruling of a tribune
PUNIC WARS	three conflicts between Rome and the city-state of Carthage, North Africa. The first (264–241 BC) gave Rome control over Sicily and Corsica and marked its emergence as a naval power; in the second war (218–201 BC) the Carthaginian General, Hannibal, was defeated by Scipio at Zama in 202 BC; and the third war (149–146 BC) resulted in the destruction of Carthage, and established Africa as a Roman province

QUINQUENNIUM NERONIS	the first five years of Nero's reign, 54 to 59 AD
RABBI	literally *my teacher*, a title given to Jewish teachers
RABBAN	literally *our teacher* – a title given to Gamaliel and others
REFRIGERIUM	a commemorative meal for the dead, eaten in a place of burial
RELIGIO LICITA	a religion permitted by the Romans
RELIGIO NOVA ET ILLICITA	a religion designated by the Romans as new and illegal
REPUBLIC	the form of government that prevailed in Rome from 509 BC, when the Romans freed themselves from Etruscan rule, until the beginnings of the empire in 27 BC
SADDUCEES	a Jewish sect, opposed to the Pharisees, whose members did not believe in resurrection
SANHEDRIM	the highest Jewish tribunal
SEPTUAGINT	a Greek translation of the Hebrew bible commenced in the third century BC, used by Hellenist Jews, and adopted by Christians
SICARII	Jewish zealots and assassins known as *dagger men* since they concealed short daggers under their cloaks, dedicated to ending Roman rule over the Jews
STOICISM	a school of philosophy founded by Zeno, BC 335–263
TALMUD	the primary source of Jewish religious law
TITULUS	a notice proclaiming the crime of a condemned person
TRIBUNE	another name for a chiliarch
TORAH	the Mosaic law
URBS LIBERA	free towns, self governing and exempted from occupation by a Roman garrison, similar to **CIVITATES LIBERAE** – free cities
VIAE	Roman roads
VENATIONES	contests between wild animals, or between animals and men, staged in Roman amphitheatres, often in gladiator shows, which originated in the second century BC and were highly popular with the Roman public
VERNACULAR	the commonly spoken language or dialect of a people or place
ZEALOT	member of an extreme Jewish sect resisting Roman rule

BIBLIOGRAPHY

Barnett, Paul	2008	*Paul Missionary of Jesus*	William B. Eerdmans Publishing Company Grand Rapids, USA/Cambridge, UK
Beitzel, Barry J	2009	*The Moody Atlas of the Bible*	Moody Publisher, Chicago, USA
Bruce, F F	1978	*In the Steps of the Apostle Paul*	Candle Books, UK
	1977	*Paul: Apostle of the Heart Set Free*	William B. Eerdmans Publishing Company Grand Rapids, USA/Cambridge, UK
	1988	*The Book of the Acts*	William B. Eerdmans Publishing Company Grand Rapids, USA/Cambridge, UK
	1961	*The Spreading Flame*	The Paternoster Press, London, UK
Casson, Lionel	1974	*Travel in the Ancient World*	Hakkert, Toronto, Canada
Chadwick, Henry	1982	*History and Thought of the Early Church*	Variorum Reprints, London, UK
Conybeare, W J and Howson, J S	1867	*The Life and Epistles of St Paul*	Longmans, Green and Co., London, UK
Cotter, Alisa S	2010	*The Interplay of Politics and Piety: Christian Pilgrimage to the Basilica of San Paolo Fuori Le Mura*	Thesis by Alisa S Cotter, Bachelor of General Studies, Wichita State University
Darby, J N	1965	*Synopsis of the Books of the Bible*	Stow Hill Bible and Tract Depot, England
		Collected Writings Expository No. 4, Volume 25, 'Meditations on the Acts of the Apostles'	Stow Hill Bible and Tract Depot, England
Denzey, Nicola	2007	*The Bone Gatherers*	Beacon Press, Boston, USA
Eastman, David L	2011	*Paul the Martyr*	Society of Biblical Literature, Atlanta, USA
Eliot, C W J	1955	*New Evidence for the Speed of the Roman Imperial Post*	The Phoenix, Volume 9 (1955) 2
Ellicott, Charles J		*A Bible Commentary for English Readers*	Cassell and Company Limited, London, Paris, New York and Melbourne
Farrar, Frederic W	1893	*The Life and Work of St Paul*	Cassell and Company Limited, London, Paris, New York and Melbourne
Glover, T R	1944	*The Ancient World*	Penguin Books, London and New York
Green, Michael	2002	*Thirty Years that Changed the World*	William B. Eerdmans Publishing Company Grand Rapids, USA/Cambridge, UK
Harpur, James and Braybrooke, Marcus	1997	*The Journeys of St Paul*	Marshall Editions, London, UK

Hawthorne, Gerald F, Martin, Ralph P, and Reid, Daniel G.	1993	*Dictionary of Paul and his Letters*	InterVarsity Press, Illinois, USA and Leicester, UK
Hastings, J (Ed)	1902	*A Dictionary of the Bible*	T & T Clark, Edinburgh, UK
Henge , Martin	1996	*The Pre-Christian Paul*	Trinity Press International, Philadelphia, USA
Henge , Martin and Schwemer, Anna Maria	1997	*Paul Between Damascus and Antioch*	SCM Press Limited, London, UK
Jeffers, James S	1999	*The Greco-Roman World of the New Testament Era*	Inter Varsity Press, Downers Grove, USA
Jewett, Robert	1979	*Dating Paul's Life*	SCM Press Ltd, London UK
Kirschbaum, Engelbert	1959	*The Tombs of St Peter & St Paul*	Secker and Warburg, London, UK
Lanciani, Rodolfo Amadeo	1901	*The Truth about the Grave of St Paul*	Fourth Gifford Lecture, 1901
Mac Donald, Dennis R	1983	*The Legend and the Apostle*	The Westminster Press, Philadelphia, USA
Massie, Alan	1983	*The Caesars*	Book Club Associates, London, UK
Miller, Andrew	1980	*Miller's Church History*	Bible Truth Publishers, Addison, USA
Morrish		*A New and Concise Bible Dictionary*	Bible Truth Publishers, Addison, USA
Morton, H V	1936	*In the Steps of St Paul*	Rich and Cowan Ltd., London, UK
	1938	*Through Lands of the Bible*	Methuen & Co Ltd, London, UK
Murphy-O'Connor, Jerome	2004	*Paul: His Story*	Oxford University Press, Oxford, UK
Neander, Augustus	1850	*General History of the Christian Religion and Church*	Henry G Bohn, London, UK
	1851	*History of the Planting and Training of the Christian Church by the Apostles*	Henry G Bohn, London, UK
Nock, Arthur D	1946	*St Paul*	Oxford University Press, Oxford, UK
Ogg, George	1968	*The Chronology of the Life of Paul*	Epworth Press, London, UK
Perowne, Stewart	1973	*The Journeys of St Paul*	Hamlyn Publishing Group Limited London, UK
Pherigo, Lindsey P	1951	*Paul's Life after the Close of Acts*	The Society of Biblical Literature, Journal of Biblical Literature, Volume 70, No. 4 (Dec 1951) pp 277–284
Picirilli, Robert E	1986	*Paul the Apostle*	Moody Publishers, Chicago, USA
Pope, R Martin	1939	*On Roman Roads with St Paul*	The Epworth Press, London, UK
Ramsay, W M	1902	*Roads and Travel in the New Testament (Article in 'A Dictionary of the Bible', J Hastings [Ed])*	T & T Clark, Edinburgh, UK
	1900	*St Paul the Traveller and the Roman Citizen*	Hodder and Stoughton, London, UK
	1960	*The Cities of St Paul*	Baker Book House, Grand Rapids, USA

Reymond, Robert L	2000	*Paul Missionary Theologian*	Mentor Books, Dublin, Ireland
Seddon, Matthew T	2010	*St Paul's Tomb?*	http://bibleversiondiscussionboard.yuku.com/topic/4758
Sharpe, Samuel	1879	*On the Journeys and Epistles of the Apostle Paul*	John Russell Smith, London
Skeel, Caroline	1901	*Travel in the First Century after Christ*	The University Press, Cambridge, UK
Slingerland, Dixon	1991	*Acts 18: 1–18, The Gallio Inscription and Absolute Pauline Chronology*	The Society of Biblical Literature Journal of Biblical Literature, Vol 110, No 3 (Autumn 1991)
Smith, James	1880	*The Voyage and Shipwreck of St Paul*	Longmans, Green and Co, London, UK
Stevenson, J (Ed)	1957	*A New Eusebius*	S.P.C.K., London, UK
Tajra, Harry W	1994	*The Martyrdom of St Paul*	J.C.B. Mohr (Paul Siebeck) Tübingen, Germany
Talbert, Richard J A	2000	*Barrington Atlas of the Greek and Roman World*	Princeton University Press, New Jersey, USA and Woodstock, Oxfordshire, UK
Tucker, T G	1922	*Life in the Roman World of Nero and St Paul*	The Macmillan Company, New York, USA
Utro, Umberto	2009	*San Paolo In Vaticano*	Tau Editrice, Todi (PG), Italy
Walker, Peter	2008	*In the Steps of St Paul*	Lion Hudson Plc, Oxford, UK
Wallace, Richard and Williams, Wynne	1998	*The Three Worlds of Paul of Tarsus*	Routledge, London, UK and New York, USA
	1993	*The Acts of the Apostles*	Bristol Classical Press, Bristol, UK
White, Jefferson	2001	*Evidence and Paul's Journeys*	Parsagard Press, Hilliard, USA
Wilson, Mark	2010	*Biblical Turkey*	Ege Yayinlari, Istanbul, Turkey
Withrow, W H	1890	*The Catacombs of Rome*	Hodder and Stoughton, London, UK
Wood, C T	1925	*The Life, Letters and Religion of St Paul*	T & T Clark, Edinburgh, UK

INDEX

Page references in *italics* denote illustrations.

PICTURE CREDITS